The
TOWER
of
LONDON
PUZZLE
BOOK

The TOWER of LONDON PUZZLE BOOK

SINCLAIR McKAY

Headline

First published in the UK in 2020
by HEADLINE PUBLISHING GROUP

1

Names have been changed to protect people's privacy.

Cataloguing in Publication Data is available from the British Library

Trade paperback ISBN 978 1 4722 7042 9
Ebook ISBN 978 1 4722 7041 2

All puzzles compiled by
Roy & Sue Preston at The Puzzle House,
except Chapter 7.

Designed by Couper Street Type Co.
Printed and bound in Great Britain by
Clays Ltd, Elcograf S.p.A

Headline's policy is to use papers that are natural, renewable and recyclable products and
made from wood grown in sustainable forests. The logging and manufacturing processes are
expected to conform to the environmental regulations of the country of origin.

HEADLINE PUBLISHING GROUP
An Hachette UK Company
Carmelite House
50 Victoria Embankment
London
EC4Y 0DZ

www.headline.co.uk
www.hachette.co.uk

CONTENTS

INTRODUCTION

ALMOST one thousand years ago, labourers on a grassy hill near the flowing Thames began work on a tower that was intended to inspire fear and awe. It began as a bright square castle of white stone with four tall turrets and was designed to remind a conquered nation that its new rulers would govern ruthlessly, and with terror if necessary. This new castle was impenetrable and indomitable.

As the centuries progressed, this original tower was joined by and surrounded with new walls, new fortifications, new towers, a wide moat and a drawbridge, forming a maze of ingenuity.

Today, almost a millenium after those labourers first slaved to construct a mighty fortress, millions of beguiled and excited visitors from every part of the world come to explore the sombre stone chambers and the winding ramparts of the Tower of London, one of the most familiar architectural silhouettes on the planet. The Tower is now, in many ways, an emblem for the entire nation: an ancient palace sitting alongside the rolling, ageless river, while behind it stand hi-tech towers of glass and steel, the financial powerhouses of the City (whose ruthless principles would have been recognised and probably appreciated by the Tower's medieval inhabitants).

The Tower's moat was drained over a century ago, but the draw-bridge across the now-green canyon is our invitation to walk back in time, through the centuries. It takes very little imagination to envisage yourself as a noble, passing the colourful Yeomen Warders – popularly known as Beefeaters. Surprisingly to some, there is not just the one tower; there are, in fact, twenty-one. The whole construction is the size of a village and, like a village, the Tower of London contains an amazing multitude of stories and secrets.

Over the course of centuries, the meanings of great landmarks can change, time and time again. Ask any child, though, about the phrase 'Take them to the Tower!' and, instantly, the images are conjured: imperious kings and queens, guards in elaborate red uniforms, and men in doublet and hose arriving by river at the Traitor's Gate, facing the prospect of a dark dungeon.

And more than this: there are other universally recognised images – aristocratic women in ruffs being led to wooden blocks, where their executioners await; prisoners facing the terrors of the rack. Then there is the rich splendour of the Crown Jewels; the gleaming martial wonders of the armoury and its historic suits of regal armour; the traditional ceremonies of the Beefeaters; and, of course, the beloved ravens, whose mere presence, according to legend, ensures the continuance of the Tower and the Kingdom.

The Tower is also a repository of enigmas and mysteries, some macabre, some breathtaking. The enduringly sinister story of the Princes in the Tower – the young boy king and his brother, reputedly done away with at the behest of their evil uncle, Richard, Duke of Gloucester – haunts and fascinates each new generation. So too does the fate of the other-worldly Henry VI, purportedly murdered as he prayed in the chapel.

But there have been other riddles too. Within these walls, historic prisoners have used the most dazzling lateral thinking to effect impossible escapes, while others developed secret codes so ingenious that their captors could not possibly fathom them.

And then there were the wild animals of the Tower, all of which brought their own conundrums: for centuries, the Tower housed an incredible menagerie, with beasts from around the world, and the keepers had to dream up ways to transport tigers or enable a polar bear to swim in the Thames.

This is why the Tower of London's history itself inspires all sorts of different puzzles, from logic headscratchers to lateral mind-twisters.

From the routes that royal prisoners were permitted to walk around the ramparts and the towers to the business of calculating the trajectories of medieval cannons, from spotting counterfeit coinage at the Tower's mint (where, for many centuries, the coins of the realm were made) to devising means of getting across the Tower's moat, here is an historic location that is, in so many ways, a puzzle box.

Nor is its story confined to centuries past, as the Tower has had its more modern uses, including the confinement of Nazis, and even the notorious Kray twins.

And some of its real-life conundrums continue to inspire fiction writers and real-life villains; the wild story of Colonel Blood, the seventeenth-century adventurer, who was the only person to devise a successful means of stealing the Crown Jewels, remains a sort of pinnacle of gentleman-thief transgression, imitated by everyone from Sherlock Holmes's nemesis, Moriarty, to a recent real-life would-be cat burglar who managed to purloin one of the Tower's keys.

Swirling around all these fantastical tales, however, are the more haunting echoes, from the many victims of the cruel regime of Henry VIII to the amazing but forlorn writings of Sir Walter Raleigh, imprisoned by Henry's daughter, Queen Elizabeth, and then, in turn, her successor, James I.

Lastly, there are the extraordinary historical turning points that the Tower bore witness to, from the organised violence of the 1381 Peasants' Revolt – which saw the Tower of London stormed – to the 1666 Great Fire of London, which came close to setting off a vast explosion in the Tower's armoury that could have wiped out the old city.

For Londoners, the Tower was a constant from the moment the turrets of the White Tower came to dominate that early medieval skyline, but, arguably, it was thanks to William Shakespeare that it came to be recognised around the nation, and on distant shores, as a crucible of history. His history plays – particularly *Henry VI* (all three parts) and *Richard III* – featured key scenes taking place within the walls of the Tower. Here was where the wheels of history turned. They never stopped.

In some ways, the casual visitor can only hope to absorb a fraction of the richness of the Tower's story in just a couple of hours, because it is a story that extends far beyond the walls of the fortress. The tumultuous events that took place in the shadow of the White Tower had consequences that rippled out well past England's shores.

Above all, the Tower of London is a treasure house of curiosities. From the arcane art of medieval bookkeeping – with coded pictures and symbols and scrolls that would keep Indiana Jones happy for months – to the strange alchemy experiments carried out by the imprisoned Ninth Earl of Northumberland; from the use of colour in interior castle decoration to early maps of the heavens, produced from the Tower's observatory, there is a beguiling labyrinth of aesthetic and scientific alleys to explore.

For some visitors, the Tower will always be axes and wooden blocks. The aim of these puzzles and conundrums and historical headscratchers will be to illuminate a rather richer and more surprising history than that. From odorous ways to keep moths away from royal robes to mouthwatering Renaissance recipes, from the poetry of aristocratic prisoners to the ghosts that stalk these flagstones by night, here is all the quirky and compelling pomp of a nation in miniature.

CHAPTER ONE

TOWERING OVER ALL

FROM THE very beginning, long before the Tower arose, London was a global city. The shape of it was established by the invading Romans around two thousand years ago, in approximately AD 43, about the time that Cleopatra ruled Egypt. And the grassy incline upon which the Tower of London was to be built had its own strategic and spiritual significance, overlooking an important river gateway to the wider world beyond.

So, the puzzles in this section are centred around the genesis of the Tower: the complexities of invasion and establishing strongholds; routes, tides, lines of attack. They are also inspired by the logic and the mechanics of early medieval construction, for, in many ways, the edifice that was to rise from that green slope by the river in the late 1070s was emblematic of a kind of ingenuity that deserves praise even today and which has helped make the Tower a World Heritage Site.

For the Romans, this new city was a vital junction of major roads and also a military base, as well as a busy trading centre. They encircled the settlement with a mighty defensive wall, a surviving part of which forms part of the fabric of the Tower today. But no empire lasts for ever. And, by the fifth century AD, after the Roman civilisation had ebbed and dissolved, people and commerce moved a little to the west, where Aldwych now stands and the old city of Londinium (no one knew for certain how it had come by that name, although there was a suggestion it had Welsh roots) was half-deserted, ghostly and ruined. Only the wall endured.

Soon after this came the Anglo Saxons, who invaded from northern Europe, and with them came a repurposing of the old city, filled now with great numbers of timbered buildings. There were no vast castles, as the nobles lived alongside the commoners. People continued to flock to London during this era, because it was still a thriving port, as it had been in Roman times, with visitors and merchants arriving from far-off lands, their boats bearing wine and silks, all docking and unloading at busy wharfs. It was a multicultural place, just as it is today, and it was commonplace to see Norman priests mingling with Mediterranean merchants. But, without any castles or forts to protect the land, it was vulnerable to attacks from invaders.

In 1066 – fated to be the twilight of the Anglo-Saxon era – a brooding warlord lurked just across the stormy Channel, in Normandy. The ferocious William the Bastard – or Conqueror, as he later became known – was a ducal warrior with a chic forked beard and a shrewd gaze (according to later portraits), and he desired the great riches – from abundant wool to rich seams of tin – that could be extracted from this island realm. He also felt, perhaps justifiably, that this land had been promised to him by the old king, Edward the Confessor, his first cousin once removed.

And so, William's boats, with their carved-dragon figureheads, made land at Pevensey, in East Sussex. King Harold, who had taken the throne after Edward's death, marched his army with some speed to the south coast to meet William. But, in a field near what is now Hastings, with limbs and heads all around being pierced and hacked, Harold lost his life. (Though possibly not, as popularly recorded, in the Bayeaux tapestry and thence through the ages, by an arrow through the eye; it is more likely he was simply torn to pieces.)

Victorious in battle, William the raging Conqueror began his progress towards London. He had to secure the city port, but knew that this cosmopolitan town of merchants would resist fiercely.

Entry into London was tricky. William's men were fought back by locals at London Bridge – the only river crossing. Unable to reach the other side of the Thames, William and his men were faced with a knotty logic problem. The Conqueror's forces were brilliant with arrows – they were far more advanced with their weapons than the Anglo Saxons – however, they wouldn't be able to take hold of London with just arrows, especially not across so vast a river, so they would need to find somewhere else to cross.

William's men were forced to march miles along the river's south bank – their every attempt to cross angrily resisted by the fierce locals along the banks. They trailed west as far as Oxfordshire, bringing vengeful fire and devastation to each village they came across, and even veering off their route to vanquish territory further south, including the royal city of Winchester. Eventually, they made it across, and William was finally ready to make a more determined lunge for London. And this time he succeeded – partly by cutting off supplies to the city. But the Conqueror made a compromise with the wealthy Anglo-Saxon guildsmen of London; unlike the rest of the country, where Saxon land was transferred directly into the hands of Norman aristocrats, fewer demands would be made upon the property of London men. Funnily enough, the London business community would always manage to be a law unto itself, throughout all the centuries to come.

In contrast to the lords of the former Anglo-Saxon kingdom, William and the Norman nobles set themselves far apart from the common folk. So, the White Tower, once it was built – together with a large number of other Norman keeps that were to be built right the way across the country – was intended to exude immense social superiority. It would take an incredibly strong army or an extremely well-organised group of rebels to attack and overtake such a construction; and the man who designed its impregnability was a learned Norman monk – a man called Gundulf of Rochester.

When it came to constructing his tower, the architect monk Gundulf immediately faced a problem: finding materials to build such an edifice was not going to be easy. London itself, a city on a bed of clay, had no indigenous stone to hew from quarries; it all had to be shipped in from elsewhere. So, for the White Tower, it was decided they would use – in part – Caen stone, brought across the Channel from Normandy. Curiously, the fearsome logistics of quarrying such stone from Caen, and then loading it on to small, unsteady boats in preparation for wild, often storm-filled crossings to the English coast, were still simpler than having it brought laboriously along uneven roads on carts from quarries far in the west or north of England, or Wales.

Builders worked upon this tower of Gundulf's for the best part of two decades, battling through gnawing frosts and humid summers. Just as now, with the London skyline jostling with attention-grabbing structures such as the Shard and the Gherkin, the White Tower, four storeys high when finished, became an extremely eye-catching feature of the Norman London landscape. Its 100ft height and its apparent impenetrability was one thing, but there was also the sophistication of its arches; an architectural flourish which impressed upon the Londoners the innate technical superiority of their new lords.

The Tower was – for its time – a fantastic powerbase. Indeed, it remains to this day unique in Europe as a complete, preserved eleventh-century fortress. The entrance was on the first floor, and, ingeniously, there were wooden stairs from the ground leading up to the door that could easily be removed in case the castle came under attack. At each corner of the square palace stood towers, or turrets, serving as fantastic vantage points; from these, on clear days, potential enemies could be seen approaching from some miles away. The north-eastern turret contained the interior staircase, tightly spiralling upwards, while the main body of the Tower was even more of a marvel, as it seemed bigger on the inside to the naked eye. As well as a profusion of arched corridors, and grand residential chambers, there was also a chapel, named after St John, which was a particularly eye-catching beauty within the towering walls. Here were pillars and arches, light beaming through tall, thin windows: a building truly fit for a king (or conqueror).

Meanwhile, in the basement of the tower a well was dug, so there was no need even to go outside to obtain water from the Thames; and as well as vast fireplaces, keeping the chambers warmed and ventilated, latrines were built into wall recesses – bare wooden boards with holes, and a long drop beneath – while one of the chambers was left windowless, in order to safely store jewels and other valuables. With an undercroft in which food and other provisions could be collected, this was a construction that was designed to withstand lengthy sieges, leaving the enemy more or less helpless outside, as those within continued to live in (relative, slightly spartan) comfort. Every resident's need was taken into account.

But William, just ten years into construction, was close to the end of his life. In 1087 he died, and so he did not see the completion of the beautiful White Tower. Could William the Conqueror ever have imagined that the building he commissioned, and with which he would always be associated, would still be standing almost one thousand years hence, teeming with visitors from around the globe?

The Conqueror was succeeded by his son, William Rufus, also known as William the Red, so called because of his rosy complexion, who very swiftly became a loathed by-word for corruption. He did not survive long and died just a few years later, in 1100, while out on a hunting expedition, when an arrow was shot through his lung (it was understood at the time as an accident, but there were assassination theories). He, in turn, was succeeded by his brother, Henry I. And it was under this new king that the Tower of London came to hold the first of its very many illustrious prisoners, and, coincidentally, it was also the first time a prisoner there came up with an ingenious escape plan.

The prisoner in question was a bishop called Ranulf Flambard. The name 'Flambard' reflected the fiery quality of his intelligence and temperament. He was instrumental in the establishment of the mighty cathedral at Durham in the north, and Flambard's lightning intellect had also made him invaluable to William the Red; he was sharp on legal arguments, especially those that made it easier for his master to gather up yet more money and other riches. But with the death of William the Red, and the ascendance of Henry I to the throne, there was a seething outbreak of anger from various nobles, who felt that they had been ill-used under William's corrupt reign, and it was Ranulf Flambard who was made to pay the price for the greedy excesses of the old regime. He was sent to the White Tower, and held captive there, his sentence apparently open-ended.

After some months of confinement within those stark stone walls, Flambard – who still had a number of allies on the outside – began formulating his scheme to trick the guards and escape the fortress. Flambard arranged and paid for a banquet (prisoners in the Tower throughout the centuries tended to pay for special provisions) in honour of his gaolers. As well as the food being brought in, there would be barrels of wine. Flambard ensured that one of these barrels would contain a length of coiled rope . . .

So, in the darkness of the evening, the fire glowing in the stone hearth, and the table creaking under the weight of succulent meat dishes, Flambard invited his guards to dine with him. Wine was poured; then more, and more again. The guards became helplessly drunk. Flambard retrieved the rope from the barrel and used it to lower himself down from a window, where an accomplice was waiting with a boat. He set sail, down to the estuary and out to France. Not all attempted escapes in the centuries to come would be as successful, as we shall see: Ranulf Flambard was one of the lucky ones.

After the initial violence of the Norman Conquest, the land soon settled into relative peace; and, in London, a great many citizens became trilingual. Latin was used not only in Mass, but also for legal affairs; French was the language spoken by the ruling class, and those who ministered to it; English, meanwhile – in its then earlier form – was the vulgar tongue of the common people, so, for the servants and tradespeople and merchants who laboured in and around the Tower, it was useful to cultivate a certain linguistic fluidity. And, with time, the French overlords, in order to make themselves understood to their underlings, were forced to learn some of their vulgar language. Thus French, Latin and Old English began – in London and elsewhere – to commingle, creating the language we know today. Visitors now come to the Tower of London from across the world, but, even in 1100, it was already a symbol of international outlook and multiculturism.

1

FROM THE FORTRESS

How many English words can you construct using the letters in FORTRESS?

* You cannot repeat letters except for R and S which can be used twice.
* Each word must contain at least four letters.
* A singular and a plural of the same word only counts as one word.
* Place names, technical, obscure and offensive words can be discarded.

2

CAEN BLOCKS

Blocks of stone were brought over from Caen to build the Tower. The challenge is to build three blocks where words read both across and down. CAEN must appear in each word square.

There is one word that will be left over. What is it?

ABLE	ACRE	CAEN	CAEN
CAEN	DISC	ELMS	ENDS
IOTA	KEYS	NEST	READ
STYE			

3

TARGET PRACTICE

Aiming arrows with the utmost accuracy was more than just a game to the early inhabitants of the Tower, as their security depended on it.

Solve the quickfire clues below and fit the six letter answers into the target grid. All answers start in a numbered space. 1 to 6 are written inwards to the bull's-eye in the centre. 7 to 12 are radial clues that go clockwise.

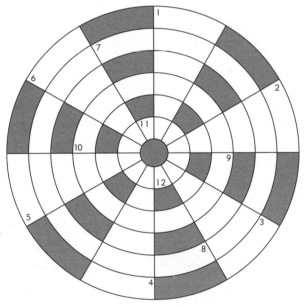

CLUES

1	A fortified dwelling	7	Watch and protect
2	Apprehend	8	Famous Tower birds
3	Tower, with a gruesome reputation	9	Engaged in conflict
4	Small knife	10	Encounter between enemies
5	Defeated	11	Guard
6	Flee to freedom	12	Material for tools or weapons

4

RECTANGLED

Here's a plan of a fortress. How many rectangles are there in the diagram?

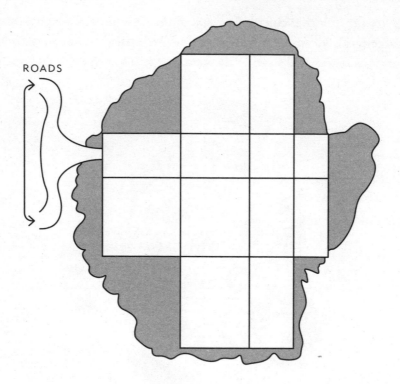

ROADS

5

WORK IN PROGRESS

Work is under way by the stonemason to complete this cuboid shape. How many more bricks are needed to finish it?

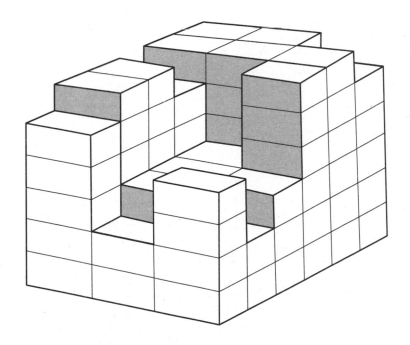

6

ARCHWAY REPAIRS

Some archways in the Tower have been severely damaged. Can you rebuild five arches from the pieces below so that they all resemble the archway shown top left?

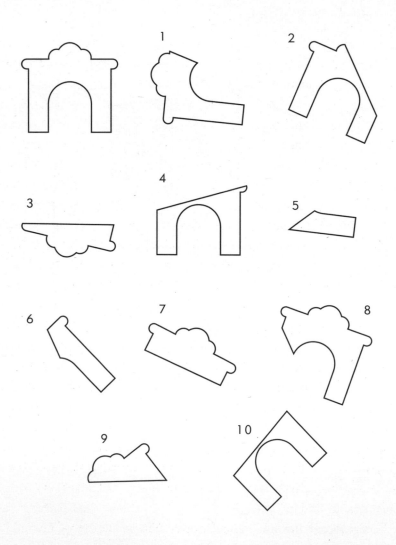

CHAPTER TWO

DARING ESCAPES
AND CRUEL CAGES

DURING THE first century of the Tower's existence, the fortress stood firm – but the city and the land around it often dissolved into blood-soaked turmoil.

After the thirty-five-year reign of Henry I ended with his death in 1135, there came King Stephen – Henry's nephew – and a period of stormy darkness known as The Anarchy. The quite sizeable problem was that Henry's daughter, the Empress Matilda, thought, not unjustly, that she had a greater claim to the throne. More than that, she was prepared to fight for it. A head-hacking civil war ensued.

Throughout these and other seismic events – including the later revolution that sowed the seeds for what became Parliament – the Tower of London became both a powerbase and sanctuary. It was fitted with luxurious trappings befitting royalty, of course, but, often more importantly, with extra defences against powerful armies, and it was certainly going to need them.

As such, the puzzles in this section will feature logic-twisters with battle themes: sieges, ladders, defences. But there will also be mind-boggling brainteasers on the theme of escape – for while the Tower developed as an elegant royal retreat, it also began in earnest its career as a sinister prison filled with anguished souls. It was at the Tower that some of the earliest examples of lateral thinking in cell getaways could be found. And it is this split identity of the Tower – part luxurious palace, part dungeon of fear – that gives its history such flavour and intrigue.

Speaking of flavour, the curiously culinary nature of Henry I's death in 1135 has continued to fascinate historians through the ages.

A medieval chronicler asserted that the cause of his demise was 'a surfeit of lampreys'. Lampreys, found in both rivers and the sea, are like a form of water-snake; sometimes larger than eels, they have hideous suckers for mouths and eyes on either side of their head. These ugly creatures were found in the Thames up until the 1800s (and, indeed, in recent, cleaner times have made a reappearance). They were considered a fine delicacy to present to royalty, and many a monarch would enjoy a feast of lamprey pie.

Quite how a king might eat so many of these snakes as to result in his death is slightly more difficult to envisage. More likely, a dish of ill-cooked lamprey brought on a violent case of food poisoning. And Henry's death made way for some shocking chicanery, with his nephew, Stephen, racing to Winchester to have himself anointed as king, while Matilda, the old king's daughter, was at the other end of the country. Was it simply the case that the nation was not ready, in the early twelfth century, to be ruled by a woman? Matilda was not popular among the rich merchants of London, it's true, but even with this being the case, Stephen had committed a rather artful medieval manoeuvre.

Through the coming centuries, the mood of London – from its aristocrats to its shopkeepers – was always the backdrop to the dramas enacted within the Tower of London. Great events somehow always linked back to that fortress on the river in some way. Thomas Becket, for example, the Archbishop of Canterbury who was shockingly murdered by Henry II's knights after the king reputedly complained of this 'turbulent priest', was, for a time, the Keeper of Works at the Tower, and Londoners took a dim view of the king's role in his demise.

Henry II's son and successor, Richard I, 'the Lionheart', the absentee king who spent most of his reign in Palestine participating in the Third Crusade, his sword steeped in blood through most of the late 1100s, decided he wanted to see the Tower strengthened during one of his rare visits home. He deputed some of his powers to William Longchamp, the Bishop of Ely, and it was Longchamp who started building additional towers around the original White Tower, with land grabbed from the neighbouring hospital of St Katharine.

Here was the first attempt at a moat – a wide protective ditch dug around the Tower, which was to be filled with water from the Thames. But, try as they might, engineers could not seem to tame or command the mighty river, and simply ended up with a muddy, smelly channel. The moat had to wait.

Rather more successful was the creation of the Wardrobe Tower. This did precisely what the name suggested: it was here that the king's rich array of finery would be stored, from cloaks to furs to doublets. This tower would also hold the king's armour, and his weaponry too. It was also the perfect place to hold the king's jewellery, thus starting the Tower's role as the repository of the most precious of the royal symbols: the crown, the orb and the sceptre.

Around the Wardrobe Tower, and the White Tower, more walls were built, expanding the precincts of the larger fortress. In addition to this, there rose the Bell Tower, which, as well as residential chambers, held great bells, intended to ring out at times of danger, ensuring the Tower's defences would be triggered, drawbridges raised and portcullises lowered. This was the earliest form of the Tower of London as a citadel in its own right.

These defences were soon tested, too: by the vile Prince John, brother of Richard I. Insanely jealous of the responsibilities and powers that had been accrued by Richard's trusted lieutenant, William Longchamp, Prince John and his forces laid siege to the Tower in 1191. Despite the Tower now being armed with vast trebuchets, ready to hurl heavy objects over the walls at crowds outside, the siege did not last long before the Tower fell into Prince John's hands: it held out a grand total of three days. Knowing that he would probably be torn to pieces by John's men, Longchamp made a discreet getaway. He was the first – and by no means the last – man to adopt drag as his means of escape. Dressed as a humble servant woman, Longchamp managed to leave the Tower and get down to the wharf, where a boat was waiting to take him across the Channel, back to his native France.

John quickly made himself comfortable in the chambers of the Tower, and having essentially usurped his warrior brother, became a quite extraordinary tyrant, not dissimilar from some of the worst *Game of Thrones* characters. It was not simply a matter of ruinous taxes – extortion, in other words – levied upon his brother's subjects, it was also his outbreaks of psychopathy. Any barons who defied him might face their children being slaughtered. In one case, a baron's family was locked up and perished before they could be released. Then there were his lustful desires: he conducted a string of extra-marital affairs, and when John's eye fell upon Maud the Fair, the daughter of a baron called Robert Fitzwalter, he demanded that Maud become his mistress.

Maud and her father protested, but John's response was to have Fitzwalter exiled to France and to kidnap Maud. This done, she was then imprisoned in a cage in a room at the top of the White Tower. Still Maud would not yield to his demands, and so the weeks passed, with the poor young woman remaining in this extraordinary state. According to some accounts, the sadistic John found his patience running out, and as her supper was being prepared one evening, he tampered with it, lacing an egg with poison. She ate it and died swiftly thereafter. Even if this seems rather too florid to be true, it is certainly the case that her father – among many other barons – longed for vengeance upon this tyrannical monarch, who had succeeded to the throne after his brother's death in 1199.

And their day eventually came in 1215, when John, facing the ire of a large number of rebel barons, reluctantly left the Tower and set sail to travel some twenty-five miles upriver on the Thames to Runnymede, there to sign Magna Carta, which, for the first time, ensured that the king was made properly subject to the law.

John met a satisfyingly unpleasant end; after attempting to go back on his agreement in Magna Carta, he sparked a civil war and the barons called for Prince Louis of France to come to England to supplant him. It was while campaigning in the east of the country, in 1216 – having emptied the contents of the Wardrobe Tower and travelling with all the royal jewels and regalia – that John's wheel of fortune turned sharply. While in transit across the marshy fenlands of the Wash, there was some sort of an accident, and it is said that the entire contents of the trunks containing the royal regalia sank irretrievably into the soupy depths.

On top of this disastrous incident, it was at around this point that John contracted dysentery. Lost in a delirium of despair one night, while staying at Newark Castle, the king ordered an eccentric banquet of peaches; he ate an enormous quantity, swilled down with a great deal of cider. All this did not help the dysentery, unsurprisingly. He died very shortly afterwards.

Prince Louis of France might well have hoped to easily claim the realm and walk blithely into the Tower of London after this, but there was an heir presumptive, John's son, the future Henry III, who, despite only being a young boy, was surrounded by loyal and strong retainers, and they moved swiftly to ensure he, not Louis, was to be the new king. As he grew older, Henry, like his uncle King Richard before him, became keen to build on the aesthetic and scale of the Tower of London. It was during his reign, in the 1200s, that the previously stern Tower acquired a new beauty and was expanded on an impressive scale.

Under Henry III came new towers: the Salt, the Lanthorn (the old word for lantern – it was at the top of this tower that lights were shone for the guidance of river traffic on the Thames) and the Wakefield. The Wakefield Tower, octagonal in shape, was especially sumptuous, as this was intended as the bedchamber for the king. There was a covered walkway connecting it to the Lanthorn Tower: this was where the queen's apartments were placed.

Contrary to the dour popular image, medieval people generally exulted in colour: churches and cathedrals were bright with reds and blues. And Henry brought a similar approach to the Tower of London. The Chapel of St Peter ad Vincula, which he had built, was finished with delicate golds and greens, and patterned walls, with the rich colours of the stained-glass windows throwing squares of purple and blue upon the stone floors. In the White Tower, he had the Chapel of St John painted, so that its ceiling was a deep red. As to the White Tower itself, the pale grey of the Caen limestone and the darker Kentish ragstone were completely transformed by the total whitewashing of the building.

The Tower of London, during Henry's reign, became an ever more conspicuous and startling structure, dazzlingly bright under blue summer skies. He also carried out vast building projects a little further west, commissioning a spectacular new Westminster Abbey, as well as a new palace of Westminster. But the Tower, with the luxurious refitting of the royal apartments, became one of the chief royal palaces. Upon his marriage to his queen, Eleanor, it was decided that this former boy king – said to have been 'crowned' with one surviving bracelet from the lost Crown Jewels – would have another coronation ceremony. And it was at this point that a new tradition began: the king and his queen staying at the Tower the night before the coronation, and then processing through the London streets, acclaimed by the crowds, as they processed to Westminster.

Henry's love for extravagant artistic flourishes was coupled with a distinctly pan-European sensibility. His mother was French, and so, thanks to her influence, he favoured a bureaucratic class composed of men from across the Channel, which resulted in English nobles being sidelined from his court. Henry was ambitious too. This was a point in time when wealthy England was extremely influential across Europe, and Henry wanted to command territories reaching far across the continent. In the years to come, his global outlook would be reflected within the walls of the Tower – from rich decorative styles for the royal apartments to some of the astonishing exotic animals kept within the fortress, of which we will learn more in the next chapter.

Henry III was succeeded by his son, Edward I, known as 'Longshanks' because of his height (and long legs); in the Tower today is a recreation of his bedchamber, complete with specially lengthened bed. He, in turn, was succeeded by his own son, Edward II, a rather less successful monarch. Edward II was not only ineffectual and corrupt, but he was hated by his noblemen for the closeness of his relationships with Piers Gaveston – who was to be murdered – and the Despenser family. Both Gaveston and the land-owning Despensers were loathed by rival barons and, to this day, it is widely assumed that Piers Gaveston and Edward II were a romantic item. Evidence for this is scanty, but, nonetheless, Edward's wife, Isabella of France, later took up with another partner – the nobleman Roger Mortimer. Prior to this, Mortimer had led a ferocious rebellion against Edward which was outnumbered and quashed, and so he had been captured and sentenced to death. This judgement was commuted to life imprisonment within the Tower. However, like many before him, Mortimer formulated a plan to escape.

Rather like Ranulf Flambard two centuries previously, Mortimer offered his guards friendly goblets of wine. The twist this time was that, instead of simply getting them drunk, Mortimer had the wine drugged with a smuggled sedative potion. With the men unconscious, the Tower's deputy constable, a man sympathetic to Mortimer who had been in on the plot from the start, got Mortimer across to the curtain wall that had been built by Henry III, then, with a rope ladder, the prisoner was able to climb up and over, down to the edge of the Thames, where a pre-arranged boat was waiting for him. Mortimer then safely made the voyage to France, where he was reunited with Isabella. The vengeful lovers then joined forces against Edward II, bringing him inexorably closer to his truly horrible end. Captured by Isabella and Mortimer's forces, he was held in a dungeon and then, in 1327, (allegedly) murdered hideously by means of a hollow horn and a red-hot poker.

Through the coming centuries, there were to be other ingenious escapes from the Tower. For example, in 1597, the Jesuit priest John Gerard improved upon Mortimer's rope ladder – and additionally threw in a prototype cypher system. His story now seems incredible. Despite facing the prospect of death for his religious beliefs, and being tortured by hanging by the wrists for hours, Gerard was incredibly clear-sighted about his getaway plan.

First, he arranged to have a gift of oranges sent to him. As a gesture of friendship and kindness, Gerard gave these to his gaolers, but asked to keep the peels. From these he made crosses – further gifts. He was then allowed to write a letter to a friend, another prisoner, who was held in the Clink prison across the river. As per the regulations, this was written in charcoal. But unbeknown to the Tower guards, Gerard had also written on the paper with orange juice he'd reserved, which was essentially 'invisible'. It was impossible to read the secret message written in juice unless one held it to a flame, at which point it would appear as the paper heated.

The message – an appeal for outside help with his escape plan – was relayed through a secret network. And one night, having loosened a bolt across a trap above the roof of his cell, Gerard climbed up and secured a rope across the moat, with assistance from his co-conspirators. The priest, a very tall man, then swung precariously, his frame inching along, while the waters rippled below. A dangerous plan, but one that proved overwhelmingly successful for Gerard, who would never again be caught by the authorities. Hiding out in country houses, and thence travelling to the continent, Gerard lived another forty years.

In 1716 there was another escape and it was, perhaps, the most enterprising and inventive – as well as amusing – of break-outs. This one involved an aristocrat called the Earl of Nithsdale, held captive in the Tower for being a part of the Jacobite Rebellion during the reign of George II.

With his fate looking dark, the Tower authorities allowed the earl the kindness of having his wife, Lady Nithsdale, visit his closely guarded quarters frequently. Lady Nithsdale was then granted permission to start bringing two of her friends – Mrs Morgan and Mrs Mills – along to these visits, to provide even jollier society for her husband. These visits were garrulous affairs, with the ladies coming and going out of the earl's room, chatting with the guards, then going back in again to fuss around him. These visits were enjoyed so much that they soon became regular social occurrences. And here was the kernel of the brilliant plan: on one of these gossipy visits, the ladies – moving to and fro – contrived to apply make-up to the earl's face and get him into a smuggled dress. In the general busy hither and thither, the guards, not paying any real attention to the ladies, failed to notice when an extra lady greeted them, handkerchief held demurely to her nose, and then left with Mrs Morgan, Mrs Mills and Lady Nithsdale.

Only some minutes later did they note the earl's absence, but by the time the alarm was raised, he was beyond the main gate.

If we cast our minds back again, to the rougher, ruder Middle Ages, ever more illustrious prisoners came to find themselves in the Tower with the long reign of Edward II's exuberant son, Edward III, which began in 1327 and lasted until 1377. Edward III's own son, also Edward, known as the Black Prince, had triumphed at the Battle of Poitiers in 1356 and brought a number of prisoners back to London, including the cream of French aristocratic society, the most prestigious of whom was John II, the King of France himself. John II's story of incarceration is shot through with medieval chivalric romanticism: among the French and the English nobility at the time, there was a craze for tales of King Arthur, and honourable knights living by pure moral codes. John II might have read one too many.

As befitted a royal, John was confined to the most elegant apartments within the Tower. But that confinement stretched on for a startling length of time. The only way out was to pay; he needed to raise a ransom for himself. So, four years later, in 1360, John II was allowed out, in order to try to find the sums demanded – and his son Louis was imprisoned in the Tower in his place, as a surety.

Louis himself had to spend a frustratingly extended sojourn within the precincts of the Tower, waiting for his father. Several years later, though, he found an opportunity to make a bolt for freedom. Alas, his own ingenious method of escape seems to have become obscured in the mists of history. However he achieved it, though, his absurdly honourable father was troubled at the disgrace that this might bring upon his own throne: the ransom to Edward III had still not been fully paid. And so, to the astonishment of his own court in France, John II returned to England and willing imprisonment, in order to make reparations for the debt.

Here, truly, was a lateral outbreak of the medieval ideal of chivalry, and it did not go unnoticed by the people of the time. Upon arriving once more in the city, John II found himself greeted with incredible warmth by the London crowds and merchants. More than this: feasts were held in the city in his honour. John remained in the city until his death a year later, after which his body was transported back to France.

There was, believe it or not, climate change even in the Middle Ages. In the 1300s, during the long reign of Edward III, temperatures in Britain fell so dramatically that the Thames froze over and crops failed. Before that, there had been vineyards in England. Now, it was often a struggle to make anything grow at all and famine ensued. That was not the only cataclysm facing the benighted population, though. There was a nasty virus that had hitherto been confined to dormice in the higher reaches of Tibet and China but which made a sudden jump across continents through a range of species. Carried now by rats and fleas, the virus infected Asiatic herdsmen, then merchants traversing the Silk Road. And so it made its way into Europe. The virus arrived in Dorset in 1348 on board a trading ship that had sailed from France. This virus was the Black Death.

Its symptoms were horrific, and there was no cure. Agonising boils and pustules would erupt all over the body; searing fever would envelop the victim; death followed swiftly. No one had immunity. The infection attacked the elderly and children with particular vigour and the population of the country was scythed; in London, half the cityfolk died. The only people who seemed able to escape this hellish disease in any way were the nobility. Anyone dwelling within the Tower of London, for example – at one remove from the teeming close-built streets beyond, and protected by walls and ditches, the river and the moat – had a much higher chance of surviving this raging visitation.

However, a few years later, one of the main repercussions of the plague would be played out within the walls of the Tower . . . But, before that, here is a range of puzzles inspired by the ingenuity and colour of the medieval period, not merely battle stratagems and escape plans, but also some of the rich texture that Henry III brought to the Tower, with the fantastically elaborate devices and decorations still to be found among the Tower's chambers.

1

KEEP SAFE

Here's a plan of a square keep with four splendid turrets on the corners. The time has come to make the keep larger so that more people and provisions can be safely protected within the walls. How can the keep be increased in size to have more floor space, but still remain square in shape and retain the four turrets on the outer walls?

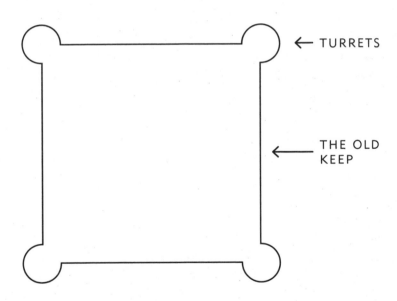

← TURRETS

← THE OLD KEEP

2

BOATMEN

Travelling by rowing boat on the River Thames was one of the best ways of moving round London.

Henry VIII saw to it that various rules and regulations were applied to the boats operating on the stretch of water. Ancient by-laws could be very complicated.

Boats leaving from the Tower could only go upstream or downstream.

It was agreed that the number of boats needed restricting and that there had to be a break in rowing after certain activity.

No boat could go downstream two boats after a boat had set off downstream.

No boat could go upstream three boats after a boat had set off upstream.

What was the maximum number of boats that could set off from the Tower wharf before there was a break in sailing?

3

ALL CHANGE

Can you see that FLAGS appear for the CROWN, and take the TRACK to the WHITE tower? Solve the random clues and slot them on the correct rungs of the ladders, changing one letter at a time as you progress.

A: C   R   O   W   N   **B:**   T   R   A   C   K

_____   _____

_____   _____

_____   _____

_____   _____

F   L   A   G   S   W   H   I   T   E

CLUES

Colour of snow

Monarch's headdress

Imperfections

Runner's course

Put pen to paper

Wrinkle the brow in disapproval

Pennants

Meaningless through over use

An instant

Glides like a river

Optical illusion

Departed hastily

4

TOWER TRAIL

Follow the trail to discover the names of eighteen towers, past and present, which have made up the Tower of London. Start in the top left hand square where we give you a letter D. The names of the towers are listed alphabetically below but it is not an alphabetical trail you seek in the grid. Your trail can take you horizontally, vertically, up and down but not diagonally.

BEAUCHAMP

BELL

BLOODY

BOWYER

BROAD ARROW

BYWARD

CONSTABLE

DEVELIN

DEVEREUX

FLINT

LANTHORN

MARTIN

MIDDLE

SALT

WAKEFIELD

WARDROBE

WELL

WHITE

D	E	B	E	W	A	E	A	U	C
E	V	O	F	E	K	B	B	P	H
R	D	R	I	E	L	D	R	M	A
E	R	R	R	A	D	A	O	R	A
U	A	O	F	L	I	N	T	D	W
X	W	W	N	T	L	A	B	M	Y
L	N	C	I	T	R	S	E	I	B
A	R	O	B	L	A	L	L	D	L
N	O	N	R	O	M	E	L	D	L
T	H	S	E	O	D	Y	W	H	E
B	A	T	Y	W	O	B	N	I	W
L	E	D	E	V	E	L	I	T	E

5

ON REFLECTION

Here's an archway standing by the River Thames. There are four details in the reflection that are incorrect. Can you spot the lot?

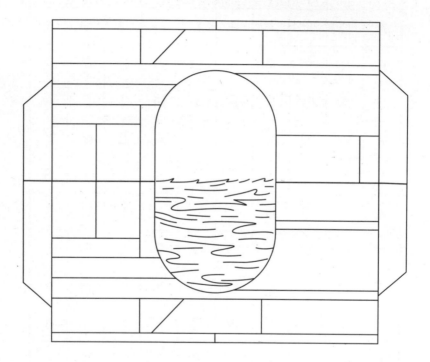

6

ESCAPES AND RECAPTURE

Down the centuries, the Tower has witnessed many daring escapes by those who have been confined within its walls. Some fugitives have fled to foreign shores, others have sadly been recaptured. ESCAPES and RECAPTURE each begin and end with the same pair of letters. Following the same pattern can you complete these words?

1   _   _   L   I   G   H   T   _   _

2   _   _   R   M   I   N   A   _   _

3   _   _   E   P   S   A   _   _

4   _   _   B   L   _   _

5   _   _   A   R   T   A   C   _   _

6   _   _   E   A   D   F   A   _   _

7   _   _   O   U   S   A   N   D   _   _

8   _   _   C   K   L   I   _   _

7

LINES OF DEFENCE

The Tower has always been evolving. New sections appear and some vanish. Plans were continually been drawn up to improve fortifications. In the sketch based on the early days of the Tower, attention has been drawn to three areas that need repair. They are shown in the squares. Can you locate where they appear on the sketch plan?

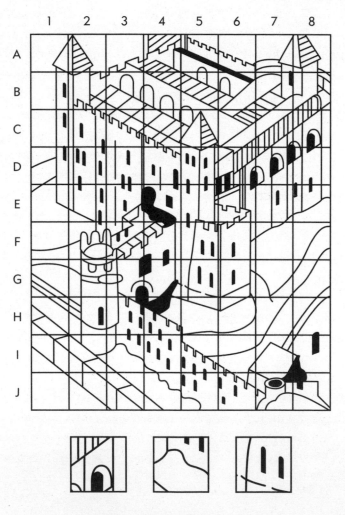

CHAPTER THREE

THE ZOO
IN THE TOWER

WHEN the excessively honourable John II of France was a prisoner within the Tower's precincts, one of his few sources of solace was paying visits to the lions kept on the western side of the fortress, and feeding them specially provided chunks of meat.

For, by that time, the Tower of London housed a colourful array of animals from distant shores in a specially constructed menagerie. Indeed, this Tower zoo endured for the best part of six hundred years, during which time a wide variety of species came to see the stone walls as their home. Granted, there were frequently tragic cases where the animals did not thrive or were not cared for correctly. However, what is striking is the ambition that saw people in the thirteenth century calculating the logistics of getting an elephant on board a river boat and sailing it across the Thames towards the White Tower.

So, the puzzles in this section will draw directly on the astounding stories of the Tower menagerie; mind-twisters concerning the transportation of leopards; how best to keep certain wild species at discreet distances; and the wisest approach when it comes to trying to coax a tiger from its lair.

The animal craze at the Tower began with Henry III in the 1200s. Not satisfied with just whitewashing stern exteriors and decorating stark interiors, this most artistically minded and globally aware monarch wanted the Tower to house creatures known only to Britons from the Bible.

The initial aim was for lions, but these were not so easily procured. Henry's father-in-law, the Holy Roman Emperor Frederick II (who ruled over territories as diverse as Germany, Sicily and Jerusalem), however, *did* have his own menagerie, which had been filled with animals captured and brought over from Africa. And so it was that three leopards embarked with their careful keepers on the voyage across the Channel and up the River Thames to become the star attractions of London's first zoo.

Unsurprisingly, they did not thrive in the Tower cell they were kept in, as no one had any idea how to keep the poor creatures properly fed, happy and healthy, and so not very long afterwards, they died. And yet the precedent had been set and Henry was undeterred. Indeed he was eager to see more marvels in his menagerie. In 1252, for example, what must have seemed like a weird vision to native Londoners arrived at the Tower, when King Haakon IV of Norway presented Henry with the gift of a polar bear.

This time, more care and thought was given to the creature's well-being and, rather than simply being kept in close confinement within the Tower walls, the bear – fitted with a stout collar and an ankle lead – was permitted to jump into the Thames, where it could hunt for fresh fish to eat. This was unintentionally wise on the part of the inexperienced keepers, who were otherwise baffled about the sorts of food that the animal might prefer, and the sight of this great creature in the Thames became a huge source of local wonder to ferrymen and those who worked on the wharves.

Several years later, the King of France decided that he too would send Henry a proud and extraordinary beast, and so it was, upon a specially adapted boat in 1255, that an elephant was transported to the Kentish shore. The elephant and its keepers first proceeded to nearby Canterbury and then walked the length of the pilgrims' way that led to London, eventually crossing the river and arriving at the Tower, where they found the specially constructed house of stone that Henry had commissioned for the animal.

Word of this dazzling spectacle spread far and fast; the medieval chronicler and monk Matthew Paris was among those who managed to get a look at the patient animal, noting enthusiastically its hairless hide with its rough skin and the mighty trunk.

By the time of Edward I, Henry III's grandson, whose long-shanked reign began in 1272, the menagerie had moved to a new enclosure, with different cells and cages and some room for animals to pace on the green. Edward also created a new position of 'zookeeper', who was officially known by the title Master of the King's Lions and Leopards. Over the years, the repeated gift of lions from various royal households in Europe and beyond proved to be perennially popular, as they were believed to symbolise the monarchy itself. It was not long, however, before they became the subject of a fearful superstition: that if the lions were to sicken and die, the monarch would similarly decline. It is said that when any lion began to seem especially elderly and infirm, it was swiftly removed and replaced with another, younger imported beast.

And some kings proved kinder to the animals than others. Whatever his grave deficiencies as a monarch, Edward II saw to it that his lions were properly fed with quartered and halved sheep on a daily basis. By hideous contrast, in the early 1600s, James I enjoyed using the menagerie for blood sports; starving mastiffs would be set against emaciated tigers, to see which animal would succeed in fatally shredding the other's flesh.

In one story, King James simply wanted to see blood flow, and so he arranged for a lamb to be lowered into the lions' enclosure on a rope, in order to witness the tiny terrified animal being eaten alive. However, it was not to be so. Upon touching the ground, the small lamb, out of curiosity, marched up to the lions, and the lions gently nuzzled it. To the king's furious disappointment, the lamb was hoisted back out unharmed.

Yet, curiously, it was also James I who, in a fit of kindness, designed a special bottle with a leather nipple from which orphaned cubs could drink milk. So he was not wholly incapable of tenderness towards the beasts. In any event, his fascination with watching animals attack one another was perfectly in keeping with the times, as there was a quite barbaric enthusiasm for bear-baiting, for example, watching a chained bear being tormented into fighting slavering dogs or armed men, and often being torn to pieces in the process. This foul practice long continued to be a hugely popular draw at specially built 'bear pits'. Such cruelty was only halted in the mid seventeenth century, after the Civil War and under the dictatorship of Oliver Cromwell – prompted by a mix of puritan religious distaste combined with a new sensitivity towards the suffering of animals – although it resumed again with the Restoration, only being completely banned in the nineteenth century.

In the Elizabethan era, the Tower's menagerie began drawing visitors other than just the royalty and nobility. Indeed, from the latter days of Elizabeth's reign, the general public were at last allowed – upon payment of a small fee – to gaze upon the animals for themselves. There were wolves, lynxes, an eagle and sometimes camels too. William Shakespeare clearly also found time to go and inspect some of the menagerie's smaller curiosities. When Hamlet is confronted by the ghost of his dead father, the spirit exclaims that his tale will make 'each particular hair to stand on end/ Like quills upon the fretful porpentine'. There was a 'porpentine' – or porcupine, possibly of the crested variety – in the menagerie at that time, so we can speculate that Shakespeare saw it with his own eyes.

As we shall see in a later chapter, in 1666 the wild animals of the Tower were fortunate to come through the Great Fire of London unscathed. Sir Christopher Wren, the visionary architect who was foremost in bringing a new London into being (most notably rebuilding St Paul's Cathedral), was commissioned to construct a completely new zoo for the Tower, with better accommodation for the various creatures, and more comfortable spaces from which to view them. This revamp was definitely necessary, as, in the summer months, the zoo was stifling; the air in the stone cells was so dense with the stink of the animals that one keeper apparently felt it 'stuffed up his head' and caused him difficulty in speaking.

Yet, amid this rankness, there were visitors who thought that the caged beasts had the power to respond to beauty. John Wesley, the founder of Methodism, spent some time thinking about the possibility that even the wildest of animals had souls. His idea for testing this proposition – on New Year's Eve in 1764 – was to visit the Tower with a flautist. If the lions were drawn to the music of the flute, then would it not prove that their inner beings were sensitively attuned to the aesthetic wonder of the world? The flute player began his rendition, but the results were disappointing. Of the five lions in the cell, four remained steadfastly on their bellies, eyes shut. Only one stood up to look around at the noise, but there was no reaction beyond this. Wesley wasn't to know that his experiment was entirely flawed and charmingly naïve; in addition, the beasts were very likely depressed, stressed and anxious. One would scarcely expect a caged human to respond with skipping delight to a flute rendition, after all.

In the new 'age of reason' that followed throughout the Georgian era, prototype naturalists were fascinated by the menagerie and the variety of species it held. In the eighteenth century, ostriches made their debut; like so many of their fellow captives, they were a complete novelty to those who came to gaze upon them. Artists came too, for here was a whole new realm of inspiration to draw from. Painters such as George Stubbs, famous for his horses, longed to master powerful representations of lions. Meanwhile, the extraordinary William Blake, whose poetry and art seemed to look into dimensions hitherto unknown, came to the Tower of London menagerie to observe the tigers closely. They provided inspiration for his most immortal line: 'Tyger, tyger, burning bright / In the forests of the night'.

Throughout the years, the behaviour of the captive animals in the Tower indicated intense distress, with the benefit of modern hindsight. Attacks upon visitors were quite frequent. In the late seventeenth century, one Mary Jenkinson, who was engaged in a romance with the zoo's lion keeper, was badly set upon by one of the animals: she reached through the cage to stroke its fur and the beast responded by chewing her arm to the bone. In those gruesome days of primitive surgery and no anaesthetic, it was decided by surgeons that her mangled arm would simply have to be cut off. The poor woman died before the operation even began.

There were incidents, too, when the leopards were seen to be waiting for their chance to launch themselves at keepers and public visitors. Meanwhile, there were other hazards: one keeper, in the act of trying to feed a bird to a vast boa constrictor, was quite unprepared for the reptile to coil itself around him, and his neck, and begin to squeeze. He was completely helpless and unable to breathe. It took two other men to desperately pull and yank at the serpent, grabbing its head and its jaws to force it to relinquish its victim.

In the nineteenth century, as the growing British empire was consolidated, increasingly exotic species, from baboons to crocodiles, were shipped back to London. Thankfully, the understanding of animals, and of how to care for them properly, had advanced significantly by then. The Georgians could now see just how very medieval this menagerie within the Tower was, and what horribly circumscribed lives the animals within were leading. Few species could hope to thrive in those conditions; and how could they be studied if they were not healthy? And so it was that the Zoological Society found a rather more suitable wide-open space for tigers to prowl and alligators to bask: the north end of the Regent's Park, at which London Zoo would be established.

As we will see a little later, the departed beasts left their mark on the Tower, both as artistic inspiration and as the source of ghost stories. But the puzzles in this section will reflect the lives of the exotic species at their starting point: conundrums and logic-twisters designed to test the ingenuity of even the most experienced lion-handler!

1

FAVOURITES

Four children have been to visit the Tower. They went on different days, and they all really enjoyed seeing the magnificent wire sculptures that depict some animals which have made the Tower their home in the past.

From the information below, can you work out the day each child visited the Tower, and which was their favourite sculpture? They all had different opinions!

The Elephant was not Catherine's favourite.

Anne liked the Polar Bear, while Thomas's favourite was the Baboon.

Henry's visit was the day after the person who liked the Lion and the day before Anne visited.

Neither of the boys went on the Monday and nobody went on Friday or at the weekend.

2
ESCAPED

Here's an inventory of animals that have lived within the walls of the Tower. These names can be found in the grid on the opposite page where they appear as a straight line of letters that can read across, back, up, down or diagonally. However hard you search there's one name that cannot be found. Which animal has escaped?

ALLIGATOR

APES

BABOONS

CUBS

EAGLE

ELEPHANT

GRIZZLY BEAR

JACKAL

KANGAROO

LEOPARD

LIONESS

LIONS

MONKEY

OSTRICH

PANTHER

PORCUPINE

PUMA

TIGER

TIGRESS

VULTURE

WHITE BEAR

WILD CAT

ZEBRA

B	A	B	O	O	N	S	G	U	W	P	Z	E	B	A
G	Y	T	H	P	R	T	R	H	E	A	U	B	O	P
E	E	C	I	A	Q	U	I	L	U	N	P	T	A	H
O	N	T	M	G	L	T	Z	G	R	T	S	E	J	R
R	I	U	E	A	E	N	Z	O	R	H	T	O	S	H
T	P	R	L	B	O	R	L	V	E	E	A	G	L	E
S	U	W	E	E	P	C	Y	Z	U	R	S	I	A	W
O	C	A	P	Z	A	T	B	P	S	L	S	S	O	L
O	R	H	H	U	R	J	E	T	O	B	T	R	S	I
R	O	L	A	S	D	S	A	D	U	H	Y	U	T	O
A	P	O	N	L	N	C	R	C	U	E	G	H	R	N
G	Y	M	T	O	D	A	A	W	K	R	D	I	I	E
N	O	I	I	L	E	C	T	N	L	A	T	G	C	S
A	L	L	I	G	A	T	O	R	P	H	L	N	H	S
K	A	W	L	E	W	M	Z	B	A	E	N	L	U	V

3

PENNED IN

Here's a beastly challenge! There are nine different types of animal. In alphabetical order they are: APE, BEAR, ELEPHANT, LION, MONKEY, OSTRICH, PUMA, TIGER, ZEBRA. There are also nine animals of each type. You have to put them in pens so that each block of 3 × 3 pens contains nine different animals, as does each row reading across and each column reading down. Creatures are indentified by the first letter of their type, with A for ape, B for bear and so on. Some have already been placed in their pens. Can you complete the task?

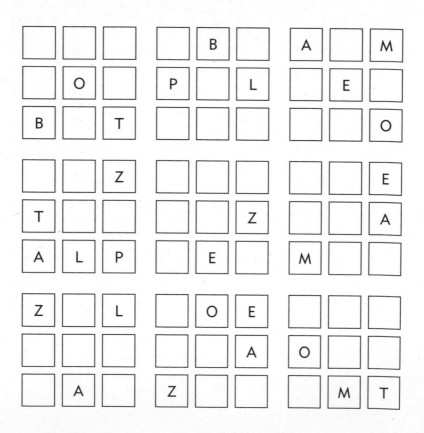

4

HIDDEN ANIMALS

The names of some exotic residents of the Tower are hidden in the sentences below. Track them down by joining words or parts of words together.

1   To see the king and queen arrive at the Tower would be a rare event indeed.

2   The Yeoman Warder entered the maze, bravely as it transpired, as he did not know what dangers lay ahead of him.

3   Even though jester Jack always makes people laugh, the lonely jester sometimes has a sad face.

4   Heralds summon key ceremony officials to perform the final duties of the day.

5   At a Tudor banquet where the monarch was host, riches beyond description were all around in the splendid rooms.

6   To ensure that her ladyship has everything she can possibly need, a personal attendant is always on hand.

5

TWO ZOOS

When the Tower finally abandoned its menagerie, the animals were rehoused and moved from one zoo to another. There are two zoos in this puzzle, for the word ZOO appears twice. Fit all the twenty-four listed words of three letters back into the grid. Words read either across or down and each word is used once.

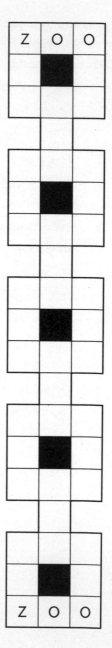

DOG	OWN
DOT	PAL
EGO	PLY
ERA	PUN
FEE	USE
FEZ	WED
FOG	WHY
LOW	YET
OAF	YEW
ODD	ZIP
OIL	ZOO
OWE	ZOO

6

ONE EXTRA

There are forty of the smaller animals housed in a series of eight cages that are built around a central stone column. There is no danger of the creatures attacking each other. There are five animals in each cage. Any warder or animal keeper could walk along the four corridors – A, B, C and D – and check on fifteen animals.

An extra creature arrives.

The arrangement must be maintained so that anyone walking any of the four corridors can still count exactly fifteen animals. What is the least number of cages you have to move to achieve this?

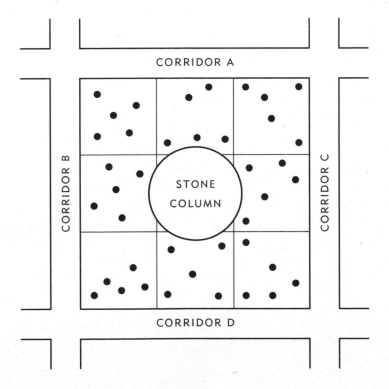

7

BEAR PAIR

Some fabulous sculptures by Kendra Haste are displayed in the Tower as a reminder of animals that lived there in the past. Here are six outlines based on a polar bear, a gift from the King of Norway. Only two are identical. Which two?

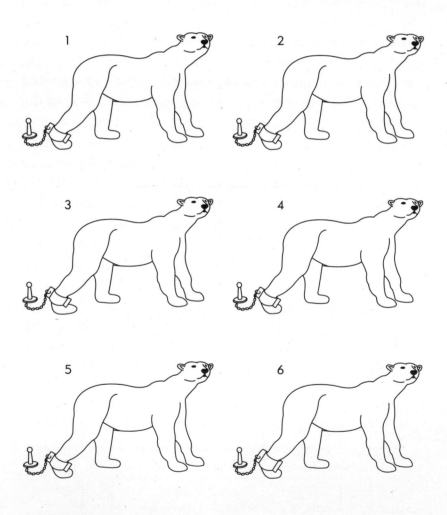

CHAPTER FOUR

KA-BOOM!

THERE was a time when gunpowder must have seemed like magic; the power to summon a storm from a few dark grains. At the Tower of London during the fourteenth century, there were lots of experiments carried out with a variety of those dark grains, in the form of saltpetre and charcoal, that resulted in more than a few unexpected explosions and singed eyebrows. In fact, by all accounts, there were rather more than a few such accidents. But it was important work. When Edward III laid siege to the Port of Calais in 1347, the Tower of London is where the royal weaponry was made and honed. The Tower armourers had already provided him with giant crossbows, and new and improved gunpowder, of which tonnes were eventually produced, was also to be deployed to aid the fight.

And for centuries after this, the Tower had a central role to play in arming the kings and queens of the realm, and providing their personal armour too. But despite the simple bloodthirsty aim of the ever ingenious new weaponry, which included everything from vast cannons to mechanised catapults, there was real craftmanship involved in bringing these devices to the battlefields of the day. As we will see, the medieval technology and finesse required to produce Henry VIII's suit of armour was so incredibly precise that, four hundred years later, NASA scientists inspected it as they formulated their first spacesuits.

So the puzzles in this section will have that flavour of weapons of yore: the design of swords, the trajectories of arrows, the length of fuses needed to detonate the explosives, the weight of cannonballs and the art not only of attack but also defence.

There was a moment in the Tower's history when it – and all those within – were suddenly incredibly vulnerable to a mass popular uprising. In the summer of 1381, villagers in Kent, and in Essex, were turning angrily on the officials who were collecting the loathed poll tax from even the poorest serfs. In an earlier age, these subjects would have been wholly powerless. But this was an unusual time. Not long before, as we have seen in Chapter Two, the land had been devastated by the ravages of the Black Death and, in some areas, half the population had succumbed to the agonising symptoms before gaining merciful release, in death, from their sufferings. The consequence of this, unforeseen by the ruling class, was that, in the years and decades to come, labour would be in short supply. If peasants found one lord unsatisfactory to toil under, they could always – in defiance of the law – move to another area, where their skills and strength were often welcomed.

The common people had also suffered through several bad harvests, and violent speculative raids from France into the Kentish countryside. The nobility, meanwhile, was trying to finance a vast war with France, and the upper classes saw no problem with heaping the burden of taxation on to those who could least afford it.

But, even among the poorest, there was literacy: because of the country's vigorous trading and commercial life, high numbers of people – certainly compared to the usual medieval stereotypes – could read and write. This meant that boiling political discontent could be expressed through verse, slogans and bills. When the official Thomas Brampton rode into the Essex village of Fobbing to collect the poll tax, and was sent packing not once but thrice, word spread, and inspired further words.

This new power imbalance was exploited most notably by Wat Tyler, a man of Kent who decided to make his stand. In Kent, tax collectors were beheaded. Further inflammatory sentiments were expressed by a dissenting priest called John Ball. Despite the name later given to the uprising, it was not just the peasantry who were revolting.

And the realm was in a vulnerable state anyway: the king at the time was fourteen-year-old Richard II. Power lay with his uncle, John of Gaunt, and with the Archbishop of Canterbury, Simon Sudbury. The revolutionaries – organising themselves brilliantly in an age when communication meant messages on horseback – assembled first at Blackheath, overlooking the distant city, and then at Mile End, down the road from the Tower, there, if their plan succeeded, to meet the boy king and make their demands: an end to the slavery of serfdom.

Among the 50,000 or so proto-revolutionaries were some whose violent rage was not so easily contained. And it was while the teenage Richard was parlaying at Mile End that a mob stormed through the main gates of the Tower. Therein they found the Archbishop of Canterbury, Simon Sudbury, and Robert Hales, the Chief Treasurer: two of the most hated figures in the realm. The two men had sought sanctuary in the Tower, together with the king's mother, because they thought it impenetrable. On that day it was not. The mobs seized the Archbishop and the Treasurer, dragged them out on to the grassy area in front of the Tower's curtain wall, and, with a terrible speed, decapitated them both. Their heads were then jammed on to pikes, and hoisted up into the air for all to see.

Meanwhile, another group had managed to break into the chambers of the king's mother, and she was shockingly harassed and assaulted. This was almost unthinkable sacrilege, and, as a result, the revolt was to end violently a few days later. Wat Tyler was knifed to death by the Mayor of London at Smithfield while talking with the young King Richard, and scores of men were hanged – even for simply voicing aloud their support for the rebels. Yet it was a turning point for the serfs, because the loathed poll tax was dropped, and, as the years progressed, the entire system of serfdom was gradually dissolved. But in the Tower of London, as a direct result of the uprising, the need to manufacture weaponry – and establish training to use it – became ever more urgent. This was about increasing the security not just for the royal household, but for this and other fortresses and castles too.

The Tower's armouries had their symbolic dimension as well. Just a few years later, when Henry IV – having seized the throne from his cousin, Richard II – assembled his knights in the Tower, he presented each of them with brand new, specially made ceremonial swords, crafted within the blacksmith's forge there. He also instigated the ceremony of what became the Order of the Bath, where the knights had to literally strip off and immerse themselves in water as a means of purification.

Strikingly, the Tower's swordsmiths at that time, working amid the glowing heat of the forges, were a married couple: William and Margaret Merssh. The husband honed the flashing blades, while the wife laboured on the exquisitely detailed handles. The armouries were also producing great stockpiles of various bows and arrows of differing designs and sizes. Indeed, Margaret Merssh had a wide range of specialities at the forge. In royal accounts from the later time of Henry IV's warrior son, Henry V, she proudly features: 'in money paid to her in discharge of 35 shillings, for eighteen pairs of fetters and eight pair of manacles, made by her and delivered by command to the Constable of the Tower of London.'

And she was something of a key Tower of London figure in the run up to – and during – the Battle of Agincourt in 1415. Henry V's preparations for this incursion into France were extensive, and a large amount of work was done at the Tower: Nicholas Mynot was placed in charge of the operation to craft thousands of arrows in readiness. But, meanwhile, in the molten heat of the blacksmith's forge, Margaret and her husband William were creating cannons and blades and other metalwork.

It was not unheard of for women in the Middle Ages to work alongside their husbands in such intensive labour. Some decades previously, Katharine of Bury had also been hard at work in the forge, her sleeves rolled up, crafting swords in the glow of the forge fire. But Margaret Merssh was quite special, as she was left in sole charge when her husband enlisted to fight alongside the king at Agincourt. Female blacksmiths had long had a slightly demonic reputation because of an age-old myth: it was said that the blacksmith ordered to make the nails that would be used in Jesus's crucifixion excused himself, claiming to have a hand injury, and that his wife stepped in to complete the task with a total absence of qualms.

The Wars of the Roses in the mid fifteenth century – the bloody struggle for possession of the throne between the houses of York and Lancaster, which, in part, inspired *Game of Thrones* – also saw the Tower armoury producing some extraordinary weapons. Some of these were ingeniously defensive.

There were caltrops, for example: an adaptation of an ancient Roman idea, involving two or three sharp iron spikes fused together in such a way that one spike would always point upwards wherever it was placed or wherever it landed. Enough of these scattered on a roadway would cause horses to buckle in their tracks.

There were also, extraordinarily, medieval bazookas: small cannons, designed to be fired from the shoulder. Again, as so often, the technology was older than might be expected. In China, from the eleventh century onwards, there had been shoulder devices for firing arrows of fire, and these consisted largely of bamboo, wicker and gunpowder. Also kept in the Tower were larger cannons, designed to fire outsize iron-tipped arrows. Ingenious and vast studded shields perforated with loopholes, which allowed them to be fired through, had also been developed: the perfect realisation of a passive/ aggressive stance.

Then there were the 'great guns': cannons developed for sieges. A century previously, somewhat primitive cannons had been used against the French. By the mid 1400s, the largest of these weapons – some five of which were kept at the Tower – could, with some difficulty, be hauled on wheels and pulled by ox to different parts of the country. By the time of the neurotic reign of Richard III, however, it was acknowledged that the French were greatly advanced in their artillery design, and so Richard had some gunsmiths brought across the Channel to the Tower to develop and build a 'serpentine' cannon for him. This type of cannon had very long, thin barrels (hence the snake reference), but with the innovation that they were pre-mounted with wheels, helping with recoil as well as with transport.

So, by the mid fifteenth century, the Tower was filled not merely with an array of bladed weapons and projectiles but also ever-growing piles of black gunpowder. When the endless head-chopping battles of the Plantagenets gave way to the equally fraught rule of the Tudors, weapons of destruction became part of a careful bureaucracy. The cannon were no less vast and spectacularly destructive, but now their handling was slightly more carefully accounted for. And the nature of battle was changing too – still hideously bloody and closely fought, but now more reliant on muskets rather than broadswords, as the new technology of the bullet and the cannonball started to supersede the blade.

Even though weaponry was developing, at the start of the 1500s there was still a lingering sense of Arthurian romance about knights on horses. And so the newly crowned Henry VIII's own suits of armour were works of artistic as well as martial wonder. They now appear on display in the Tower, and are among the most eagerly sought-after attractions for visitors, almost as though they are shells in which we can all imagine the living, breathing king, as though he were still here with us now.

In his youth, Henry VIII had been slim and athletic, and the armour made for him at that time reflected that. The suit that was made for Henry to wear to the 1520 meeting with the King of France at the Field of the Cloth of Gold is an aesthetic wonder in its own right. This was an occasion at which tournaments – themselves another throwback to the Arthurian romances – were contested. Henry, then twenty-nine, and 6 foot 2 inches, had a suit of foot armour (that is, armour specifically intended for tournament contests on foot) constructed. The silver parts were interlocked and interlaced in such a way that mobility was maximised and yet not an inch of flesh was exposed. The headpiece could rotate upon a collar, which was, in turn, flexibly secured to plates for the chest and the back. Even the extremities, such as the toes, were encompassed, in bear-paw-like moulds. The codpiece – fashionably large – was later to draw the attention of countless visiting nobles who saw the suit on display. There was an almost absurd element of boastfulness about it. But even the most encompassing armour of the time left a few small gaps or vulnerable points, simply in order to allow movement. And yet here was a suit of armour that was both a technical as well as an artistic triumph, a feat of engineering. Its weight of almost 100 lbs was testimony to the young king's physical strength at the time.

And the technical brilliance endured through the centuries. In 1962, engineers from Garrett AiResearch, working for NASA on the space programme, became interested in it as they were fathoming means to create suits that could withstand the icy vacuum of space. Directed to the Tower of London by the New York Metropolitan Museum of Art, these engineers were fascinated by the Tudor solutions to a metal suit where all parts interlocked perfectly, allowing amazing fluidity of movement. Indeed, quite recently, NASA sent one of the Apollo spacesuits to be photographed alongside the 1520 armour; an exquisite illustration of the gulf between centuries being bridged.

Different suits of armour also reflected Henry's later, fatter years. The 'Wilton' suit is much more bulky and, indeed, must have taken fantastic effort for the corpulent and deeply unwell monarch to wear.

As battle evolved through the coming decades, the chief projectile used moved from arrows to bullets; soldiers in the seventeenth-century English Civil War were issued with much less cumbersome helmets and breastplates, some of which can still be found in the Tower today. Mighty suits of armour spoke of a world long vanished.

Gunpowder, however, continued to be one of the Tower of London's most prolific products. Even gunpowder that was not made within the Tower's walls was stored there, in vast barrels. When, one night in September 1666, a fire in a bakery in nearby Pudding Lane began to spread through the close-built, claustrophobic timber-built streets of the city, the initial reactions from authorities such as the Lord Mayor were dismissive (he vulgarly suggested that a woman might be able to douse the blaze simply by urinating on it). But, over the course of the next two days, the fire spread so far, and became so intense, that it started altering the very chemicals in the air itself.

Oxygen was sucked into the blaze, while the hot winds carried blazing fragments of wood and other materials, which then sparked further fires, which in turn intensified the inferno. At last King

Charles II was informed; but what was to be done about the huge stores of gunpowder in the Tower that the blaze was heading towards?

The vast roaring fire, flickering over the rooftops, and consuming so many cherished medieval landmarks throughout the maze of city lanes, could not be fought with water, for no machinery existed that could pump sufficiently strong hoses. The other traditional tactic – simply demolishing all the houses and shops that stood in the path of the oncoming flames – was having only limited success. If the flames reached the storehouses in the Tower, the resulting gunpowder explosion would most likely have destroyed the White Tower – and indeed, a great deal of the City around it – in a split second. But the Great Fire's ineluctable advance, just yards from the outer walls, at last began to stall, the fire's momentum at last having exhausted itself. The Tower had been spared, almost by a miracle. Outside its walls, much of the flame-gutted city had to be rebuilt, though now in brick and stone.

By the end of the seventeenth century, the Grand Storehouse at the Tower featured an extraordinary collection of antique armour, longbows, muskets and other weaponry, and had become a powerful draw for visiting foreign dignitaries. And so it became more of a museum than a working store, as the Tower continues to be today.

The Board of Ordnance continued to meet at the Tower of London until the early nineteenth century, whence it moved closer to the Palace of Westminster. Since then, though, there has always been something curiously pleasing about the idea that any weapon of war is doomed, in the end, to become obsolete and end up as a museum exhibit. The puzzles in this section pay homage, if not to the destructive instincts, then to the ingenuity of those who calculated cannon trajectories and honed the noblest blades. It might seem esoteric knowledge now, but those weapons had not only elegance but were also made with mathematical skill.

1

CHAIN MAIL

Chain was part of a suit of armour and consisted of interlocking pieces of metal for protection. Choose the correct word from the list below so that you can link the words from top to bottom, linking CHAIN to MAIL. Each word links to the word before it and connects to the word following it. There is one word which will be left over at the end as it doesn't fit. Which word is it?

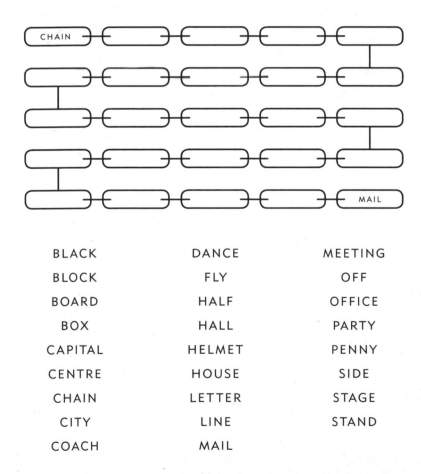

BLACK	DANCE	MEETING
BLOCK	FLY	OFF
BOARD	HALF	OFFICE
BOX	HALL	PARTY
CAPITAL	HELMET	PENNY
CENTRE	HOUSE	SIDE
CHAIN	LETTER	STAGE
CITY	LINE	STAND
COACH	MAIL	

2

JOUSTING

Two knights are taking part in a jousting contest. Armed with a lance and mounted on horseback, the two combatants face each other. The Red Knight starts from the west of the field while the Black Knight starts from the east. Moving from opposite ends of the tournament field, they travel in straight lines coming towards each other. The jousting area is measured out in yards. The horses gallop at a constant speed but the Red Knight is faster than his opponent. The riders first come together 37 yards in from the east. They parry, ride to the end of the track, then turn round and head straight back towards each other. When they meet the second time, they are 21 yards from the west.

What was the length of the jousting area in yards?

3

BULL'S-EYE

The quickest way to score exactly 100 is to land one single arrow into the bull's-eye in the centre of the target. How many arrows do you need to find another way of making 100?

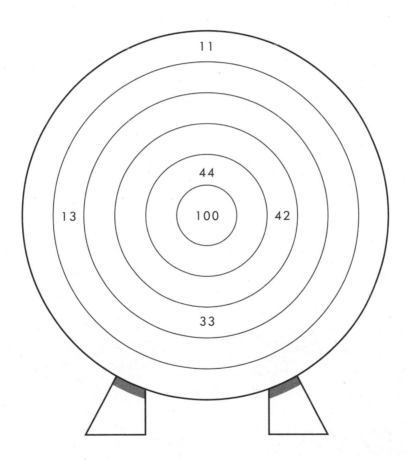

4

ARMOURY AWRY

Someone has been making mischief in the Armoury as the labels for a number of weapons have had the letters in their names muddled up and made into different (and clearly inaccurate) words. Can you sort out the muddle and make the labels correct again?

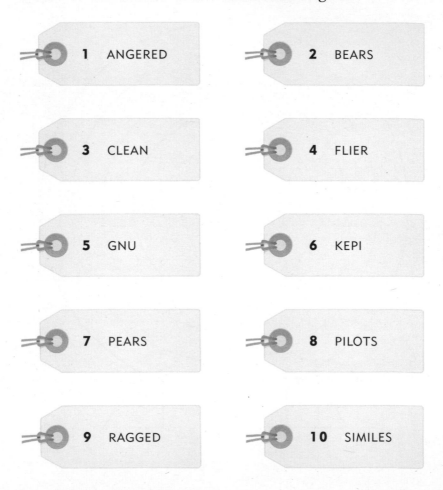

1 ANGERED

2 BEARS

3 CLEAN

4 FLIER

5 GNU

6 KEPI

7 PEARS

8 PILOTS

9 RAGGED

10 SIMILES

5

LOITERING WITHIN TENT

No self-respecting knight could go to battle without taking his personal tent with him as a place to rest between skirmishes. Which of the pieces of cloth, below, was designed to build the 3D canvas tent shown at the top of the page?

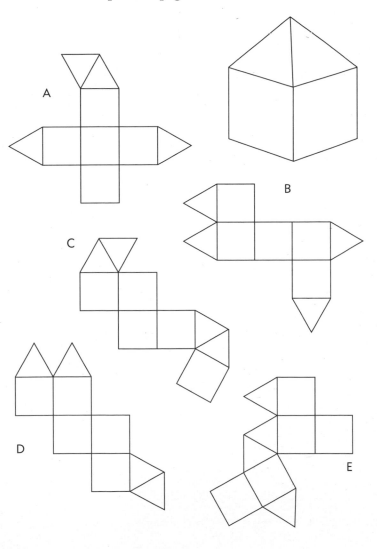

6

READY FOR BATTLE

Dressing a knight for battle was no simple task. The many items of armour had to be fitted to the body with the utmost precision. In this puzzle the words associated with armour have to be fitted back into the grid with the same accuracy. Words can read across or down and interlock crossword-style.

Four letters
BELT
COIF
IRON
LINK
SPUR

Five letters
BEVOR
METAL
RINGS
RIVET
STEEL
VISOR

Six letters
CUISSE
GREAVE
HELMET
TASSET

Seven letters
HAUBERK
SABATON
SURCOAT

Eight letters
PAULDRON
VAMBRACE

Nine letters
GAUNTLETS

Twelve letters
BREASTPLATES

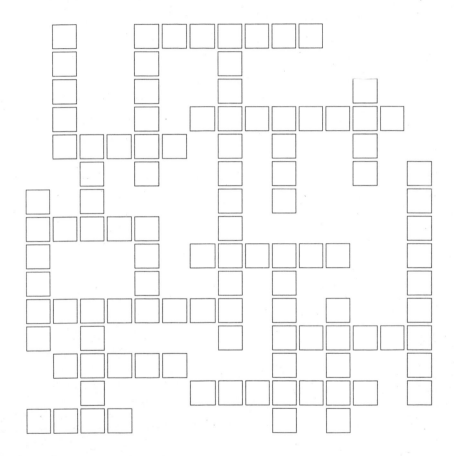

7

UNDER SIEGE

Since the fourteenth century the threat of revolution has caused concern within the Tower walls. In the map below the Tower is being besieged by no fewer than eleven groups of rebels; the Attackers, the Battlers, the Cavalrymen, the Deadliest, the Escapees, the Fighters, the Guardsmen, the Hardiest, the Ironsides, the Jousters and the Kingsfollowers. If all the groups follow the directions of the arrows, at which of the marked eleven locations near the Tower, 1 – 11, will three groups meet and therefore have a greater chance of taking control?

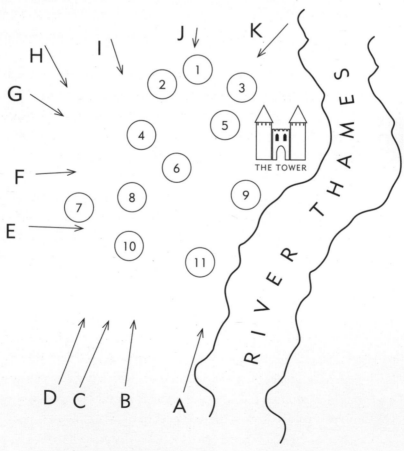

CHAPTER FIVE

THE SHADOW
OF THE AXEMAN

THE MACABRE paradox of the Tower of London is that, in addition to being a place of safety for royalty and the elite, it very often turned into their place of execution. It cannot be denied that this is a significant part of the historical frisson that the fabric of the fortress carries today. All visitors are intrigued by the thought that here was where dukes, princes, chancellors, a king and several queens met their terrible end.

The stories are so familiar, so woven into the tapestry of British history, that they seem almost cartoon-like. Indeed, in the early 1970s, there was a *Carry On* film that turned the grim spouse-killings of Henry VIII's reign into a bedroom farce. But to examine these murky stories now is to shine a bright light into the late medieval mind and it helps us focus on how the Tower came to acquire such an ominous dimension in the public imagination. The puzzles in this section will explore the cryptic meanings of communications between prisoners and loved ones and will unearth the buried clues and meanings in letters, testaments and in the messages scratched into the stone of cell walls.

Those tangled and maze-y years of the Wars of the Roses were where a lot of the trouble began. In 1471, the unwell fifty-year-old King Henry VI was on the throne. Untypically for monarchs of that period, he was a gentle man who seemed paralysed and terrified by the crown and all of its responsibilities, which he had inherited aged just nine months old, when his warrior father, Henry V, died. He thought that the Tower offered a form of sanctuary, especially at a time when no nobles in the land were safe from the hacking swords of civil strife. However, unfortunately for Henry VI, there was an aggressive usurper, Edward of York, soon to become Edward IV, who was intent upon seizing the throne and the succession. But it was not by this usurper's hand that Henry would meet his bloody death.

For some years, King Henry VI had been prone to catatonic trances, unable to respond to those around him; the exact nature of his mental health problems is still debated today. He lived frugally and rejected the sumptuous trappings and wealth of the Crown in favour of a basic life of devotion. Some said he dressed 'like a farmer'. Perhaps in another age this modesty might have found favour with the court, but Henry had a strong aversion to violence in any form. Consequently, this attitude led to many others feeling anxiety about the future well-being of the realm, especially since it was always vulnerable to attacks from its neighbours on the continent.

The previous year, 1470, after decades of internecine war between aristocratic families, the king, with his household, had been forced to flee to Scotland, but, in one of those sharp reversals that marked the tumult of the period, they were captured by forces loyal to Edward of York. But there was another revolution of that wheel of fortune to come: Edward IV, in turn, was then forced to flee to France by another faction of nobles, having made an extremely unpopular marriage alliance with Elizabeth Woodville and her ambitious family. In 1471, Edward returned, hoping to definitively conquer and replace Henry on the throne. After a ferocious fight, however, he was slain at the Battle of Barnet.

The restored and saint-like King Henry VI remained voluntarily within the precincts of the Tower and took great comfort in the Chapel of St Peter ad Vincula. But it was in the Tower that he met his end, in a demise fogged in mystery. There were some who assumed that the death of Henry's son, Edward of Lancaster, at the Battle of Tewkesbury in 1471 brought on a deadly attack of melancholia. But, in *Henry VI, Part III*, William Shakespeare depicted a much more chilling scenario.

The mild king is walking the Tower battlements reading a Bible when he is met by the 'crookback' villain, Richard, Duke of Gloucester, a 'bottled spider' (Shakespeare's dramatic portrait of Richard has never stopped overshadowing the real man). Henry knows instantly why Richard has come and what he intends to do, comparing himself with a sheep about to have its throat ripped out by a wolf. In his closing peroration, Henry curses Richard, and Richard cuts him off curtly by knifing him repeatedly.

The story had an extra layer of verisimilitude because of Shakespeare's treatment of another of Richard's alleged murders, as we shall see very shortly. But whatever the truth of the matter, the King's Chapel in the Wakefield Tower becomes a shrine on 21 May of every year to mark the anniversary of Henry's death. The chapel is where representatives of Eton College and King's College, Cambridge – both founded by Henry VI – gather for a service, called the Ceremony of the Lilies and Roses, in his honour.

The alleged murder of Henry VI, whoever was responsible, did not, however, leave the path to the throne clear for Richard, Duke of Gloucester, and that progress was made immortally lurid by Shakespeare, in *Richard III*, with his anti-hero plotting and murdering and gloating his way towards the Crown. Among the victims was his own brother, George, Duke of Clarence. Still disputed today is the exact manner of his killing. On trial for treason and for see-sawing allegiances, Clarence was being held prisoner in the Tower of London. According to chroniclers at the time – and then, later, according to Shakespeare – the duke was stabbed, then drowned in a butt of malmsey. A butt was a vast barrel and malmsey was a sweet and much sought-after white wine. The slaying was the chilling illustration of Richard's utter ruthlessness (even though there are those who suggest that, if he did indeed drown in a barrel of white wine, there are worse ways to go).

The most notorious and chilling of the murders attributed to Richard III, however, were those of the 'Princes in the Tower', Richard's young nephews. The princes were thirteen-year-old Edward

– who was to become Edward V, after the sudden death of his father, Edward IV, in 1483 – and his ten-year-old brother, Richard, Duke of York. Their uncle, Richard III, initially muscled in as Royal Protector, since Edward was still so young. Richard had Edward transferred to the Tower of London. In theory, it was to provide a secure home until the boy's coronation at Westminster could take place. But the coronation day was postponed; and Richard persuaded the boy's mother to bring Edward's brother to the Tower as well, so that he would have company there.

In some accounts, as Richard further entrenched his protectorate power, the boys were seen often on Tower Green, engaged in games. But as the days went by, they were moved further within the precinct and finally into the White Tower. It was said by some that young Edward was now very much aware of the mortal danger that he was in and that the boy spent a great deal of time in the White Tower's chapel, in earnest prayer.

The arguments about what followed are still rehearsed passionately today. Thanks largely to Shakespeare, the assumption is this: that the wicked Richard, now having seized the crown for himself, had the children murdered. How? Richard managed to persuade the Tower authorities to relinquish the keys to his nephews' room for one night, Shakespeare alleged. Assassins were sent to the Tower and suffocated the boys in their beds with their pillows.

This is one theory. Other recent suggestions are that the boys were able to escape, and live their lives under new identities. But the truth is that the boys were simply never seen again; and Richard III embarked upon his bitterly short-lived reign. He had the princes declared illegitimate, should anyone try to use them as a lever to destabilise his reign, but this only deepened suspicions. In France, he was denounced as the killer of the boys. And, indeed, the rumours spread around England, causing tremors of public revulsion, and imaginative sympathy for the poor children. Vicious though the Wars of the Roses had been – heads hacked off and jammed on spikes without a thought – no one else had descended to quite these stygian depths.

Come the Battle of Bosworth Field, Richard III was killed. His remains were lost; and it was only a few years ago that they made their startling reappearance, having been exhumed from underneath a car park in Leicester. Richard had been defeated by Henry Tudor, soon to be Henry VII, once he claimed the throne. He was the last Lancastrian, and had fled the country some years previously. But the new King Henry had a problem. If the boys were actually still alive – complete certainty was not possible, since there were no bodies – then the young Edward's claim to the throne would be unanswerably stronger than his own, even though he had married their sister. It was certainly convenient for Henry VII too that the boys were out of the picture.

The continued speculation surrounding what happened to the boys, mainly pointing the finger at Richard of Gloucester, seemed persuasive. According to Sir Thomas More, who was writing a few decades afterwards in the early 1500s, the bodies of the boys were buried at the foot of one of the stairwells in the White Tower. An early form of urban legend, one might suppose, save for the fact that, in 1674, during some building work, the skeletons of two boys were indeed found beneath the stairwell. Richard's reputation as a cold-blooded killer was cemented for the ages. The remains were interred in Westminster Abbey, and, following some rudimentary tests in 1933 (revealing microscopic traces of velvet, suggesting that the bones were indeed aristocratic), his guilt has been the assumption ever since.

By the time of the reign of Henry VIII, the second Tudor monarch, the dual nature of the Tower – both opulent royal residence and terrifying prison for nobles facing death – was well established. Its most famous victim is Anne Boleyn. She was more than simply Henry VIII's second wife, as she played a crucial role in changing the course of British – and European – history.

Henry, handsome and athletic when young, had been married to Catherine of Aragon for twenty years, but the marriage had produced one surviving daughter, Mary. This was an age in which childbirth was hazardous and in which the need to conceive a legitimate royal male heir was a matter of national neurosis.

There is a suggestion that Henry's eyes first alighted on Anne Boleyn, the daughter of Sir Thomas Boleyn and Elizabeth Howard, when she played the allegorical figure of 'Perseverance' in a court masque. The masque was a form of theatrical amusement involving various ladies, with their assigned 'virtues', defending a 'castle' against knights with other qualities, such as 'Ardour'. The young lady representing 'Perseverance' had come forcibly to the attention of the king. 'Mine own sweetheart', he wrote to her.

He might have wanted her as a mistress, but Anne was not interested in this. Henry was determined to marry her, but, as a Catholic, he would require permission from the Pope to divorce Catherine of Aragon. Such permission was adamantly not forthcoming and so Anne Boleyn pressed a radical text into Henry's hand. It was William Tyndale's *The Obedience of a Christian Man*.

The revolutionary Tyndale thesis was that authority lay not with the Pope in Rome, but in the actual text of the Bible itself. After all, were these not the words of God? Henry had been using Cardinal Wolsey to try to broker an agreement with the Pope, but the Cardinal had failed and died shortly afterwards. In 1531, Henry broke up with Catherine regardless and, in 1533, he married Anne. The rupture with Rome was underway; the authority of the Catholic church was no longer recognised in England, even though Henry was devout and continued to observe the rituals.

Anne soon had a daughter, Elizabeth, but afterwards came a terrible sequence of miscarriages. On top of this, the marriage was viewed with hostility throughout Europe, and most certainly among many of the senior courtiers around the king, who never ceased their plotting against her. Henry became convinced that the marriage was unlucky, or accursed, and those around him prepared to frame Anne, accusing her, and various associates, of treason and plotting against the king.

And so it was in 1536 that Anne was taken to the Tower, arriving by river and entering through Traitor's Gate. The apartments where once she had resided before her coronation as queen consort were now her gaol. Her execution is an occasion that has passed into a form of legend, because of her display of courage when commenting on the skill of the executioner, and upon the fortunate fact that she 'had only a little neck'. She was beheaded with a sword on Tower Green and, as we will see later, there were subsequent haunting stories that her spirit never left the Tower.

It was only a matter of some four years later when Henry's fifth wife, Catherine Howard, was awaiting precisely the same fate. The crimes she was accused of involved adultery and promiscuity, but at this stage in the king's life, it is more than possible that Henry VIII's sanity had been corroded by his physical infirmity. He was huge and gross, with legs that wept with foul-smelling ulcers. It was alleged that Catherine had had an affair with the Keeper of the Wardrobe, Thomas Culpepper, and, indeed, under torture he confessed to this. Added to this were rumours concerning her pre-marital sexual relationships with her music tutor, Henry Manox, and a family associate called Francis Dereham, who had boasted that, if the king were to die, he would marry her. Catherine too faced the executioner's block on Tower Green.

This entire period, with the Tower as its symbolic backdrop, now fascinates historians precisely because this was a society of great artistic sophistication and intellect, co-existing with this extraordinary bloodthirsty barbarism. To be near the king was to be in constant peril for one's own life. The plots and schemes of rivals, combined with the increasingly sociopathic rages and passions of the monarch, meant that not even the most brilliant and valued advisers were safe.

Henry's marriage to Anne had caused one of the most famous crises of moral conscience in British history. The Lord Chancellor, Thomas More, while accepting the king's second marriage, could not bring himself to sign or swear to the Oath of Succession, which would cement the royal line and the place of any of Anne's children within it after Henry's death. The difficulty was that the oath meant denying the supremacy of the Pope, and More could not do that. The king's adviser, Thomas Cromwell, worked up a dubious case against

More and, in the end, the ascetic – but witty – lawyer was taken to the Tower. He too entered through Traitor's Gate, where the lieutenant, Sir Edmund Walsingham, greeted him and, as tradition demanded, asked for his toppermost garment. More wryly handed over his hat, but Walsingham had meant his gown.

There is some ambiguity about where in the precincts his cell was located. The most likely contender was in the Bell Tower. Here was a room that was both spartan and yet somehow grand: it had a high vaulted ceiling, a plain table and stool, a pallet bed, a fire, and a narrow open window. It would have been extremely cold almost all the year around, as the stone walls were several feet thick and there was no protection from winds or frosts.

More was allowed the use of the chapel and he spent much of his days in prayer and meditation. He was eventually allowed the use of writing materials and devoted time to composing essays and fables, some of a religious nature, and some slightly more fantastical, such as tales of people arranging to have their heads cut off for differing reasons.

A fellow prisoner, John Fisher, the Bishop of Rochester, was locked up at the same time, and for broadly the same reason: refusing to accept Henry's supremacy over that of the Pope and the Catholic church. He and More – though only a short distance from each other in their individual cells – wrote to each other frequently, the letters carried to and fro by the Constable of the Tower. Mindful of potential sedition, and the dangers for anyone of being implicated, More had each letter burnt after it was read, declaring that fire was the best store for such correspondence.

But what a life of fear this was for the former Lord Chancellor, who, at the end of each day, preparing for his uncomfortable pallet bed, would wrap himself up in a linen sheet and pray for sleep that was almost impossible, simply because, in the dark, the possibilities of horrific execution loomed ever larger.

He was allowed visitors, in the shape of his daughters and his wife, who, in vain, tried to persuade him to back down. Surely better to simply swear a simple oath and live than face being killed before a crowd? But More could not countenance it. Not because he was exceptionally brave – indeed, he confessed that this was 'the weeping time', and his terrors were plain to see in his writings – but because he genuinely could not reconcile himself to accept this new realm. He struggled, with his nightmares, to prepare for the next realm instead.

More was at least spared the more terrible sentence of being hanged, drawn and quartered. This was the most sadistic and extraordinarily gruesome method of execution, involving the body being torn inside out. More was lucky, in that he was sent to face the axeman for a swift death. The scaffold, as ever, was upon Tower Green, overlooking the main fortress. More faced his day of doom with brittle-dry humour, asking that the axeman help him up on to the scaffold, but not to worry too much about him coming down again, which he would see to himself.

Not long after Thomas More's execution, King Henry VIII's disfavour fell upon the previously indispensable man who had done so much to make all the previous executions possible. Thomas Cromwell was ignominiously arrested at a council meeting in the summer of 1540, accused of treason and heresy. He was stripped of his symbols of power (his chain and garter) and of his title, the Earl of Essex, and found himself conveyed to the Tower. He had advised the king on his fourth unsuccessful marriage, this time to Anne of Cleves. The king, in his increasing ill-health and malevolence, had become paranoid about the man to whom he always turned. This was a sharp and vertiginous fall for Cromwell, not merely from the comforts of his family home, but also from the position of arguably the most influential man of the age. And his own terror was great; he saw no need to try to hide it. He was already extremely familiar with the Tower, and he knew that the chance of his leaving was remote.

Rather than the austere vaulted cold of More's cell, there is a theory that Cromwell was confined to the Queen's Apartments, which had originally been fashioned and furnished for Catherine of Aragon, and used by Anne Boleyn prior to her coronation.

It was from this prison that Cromwell – unlike his old foe, More – tried to save himself. He wrote again and again to the king, desperately trying to impress upon him his loyalty and explain the baselessness of the charges against him. Henry by this time had his eye on his sixth wife to be, Catherine Parr, but with his fatty veins still roaring with disease, and his flesh still puckered with decay, the courting had a more fevered quality and his moods became ever more volatile. He simply pretended that Cromwell had never existed. Cromwell's final letter was the most extraordinary plea from the heart: 'Most gracious prince, I cry for mercy, mercy, mercy.'

There was none. And on the day that Henry married his sixth bride, Cromwell was taken to the same scaffold as those luminaries before him. He was gracious in his acceptance of his fate, using his final words to reaffirm his loyalty to his king. It took three agonising blows of the axe; and then Cromwell's body was laid to rest, with some irony, adjacent to that of Thomas More and Anne Boleyn, in the Chapel of St Peter ad Vincula.

The postscript to Henry's fear-filled reign came in the violent period following his death, when claimants to the throne were sequentially seized and sent to the Tower. Most famous is Lady Jane Grey, queen of the realm for just nine days, and installed to try to prevent Henry's eldest daughter, Mary, getting the crown. Mary was Catholic, and after the revolution of the Reformation, the idea of the kingdom pivoting back to Catholicism was too much for many nobles. Lady Jane Grey was the seventeen-year-old great-granddaughter of Henry VII, and so Henry VIII's great-niece; she had a lively intellect, and a taste for studying Plato.

Her short-lived rule came to be when Henry's son, the child king Edward VI, who had succeeded his father to the throne, realised that he was dying and decided to disinherit his half-sisters, Mary and Elizabeth, in the hope of being succeeded by a Protestant male, or if that were impossible, by his cousin Jane Grey. There were no protestant male successors at the time of his death, so Lady Jane, after receiving the news in some confusion, sailed in reluctant splendour from Syon House upriver on the Thames to the Tower, to prepare for her coronation. She was later joined by her eighteen-year-old husband,

Lord Guilford Dudley, heir to the dukedom of Northumberland, and her parents.

For her coronation, the young queen to be was bedecked in a white jewelled head-dress and a green velvet dress shot through with gold, together with rubies and diamonds. The royal party processed from the Tower to Westminster, but Jane initially refused to accept the crown, horrified by the position she was being put in.

After this hesitation, her coronation proceeded as planned. But already the Privy Council was being besieged by an enraged Mary Tudor, demanding the crown for herself. Jane's supporters raised an army, but Mary's army was bigger, and Mary, as the daughter of Henry VIII, had huge support throughout London and the land, despite her Catholicism. So, after just nine days, the young Queen Jane was overthrown and the Tower became Jane Grey's prison. Another fatality in that pitiless era – the young woman and her young husband both went to the block.

When the time came for the twenty-year-old Elizabeth – Mary's half-sister, and Anne Boleyn's daughter – to make her own enforced voyage along the river to the Tower, she was keenly aware of the terrible danger that she was in. Mary was trying to prove that her half-sister had been actively plotting to take the throne, but Elizabeth's allies were staunchly defending her, even under pain of torture. Arrival at the Tower, however, did nothing to daunt Elizabeth's fiery spirits, which were evident from the moment her boat glided through Traitor's Gate. She got out at the water's edge and sat in the lapping tide, refusing to move, while proclaiming that she was anything but a traitor. She was then escorted by means of stony and patient persuasion to an especially comfortless cell in the Bell Tower. Her privileges and rights were scant, but among them was leave to walk around on the rooftop of the Bell Tower and the tower linked to it. The area, still existent, is now called Princess Elizabeth's Walk.

Elizabeth's fury was further stoked, meanwhile, when the food that her supporters had sent her was continually interfered with by the Tower guard; either checking it for secret messages, or filching the finest cuts of meat. The princess persuaded the authorities to allow her own cooks to prepare the food on the Tower premises, in one of the great kitchens.

The interrogation of her friends continued, and Mary's Privy Council were raptor-eyed for any nugget of evidence that might lead the potential usurper to the executioner's block. But, after two months, there was nothing and Elizabeth was instead transferred to another place of confinement – Woodstock, deep in Oxfordshire. The future queen was one of the very few from that period to have been released from the Tower intact.

What seems quite extraordinary now about all these doomed souls, over the span of the ages, is how those who lived and worked around these prisoners in the Tower accepted this side of the fortress's life. In one corner, a menagerie; in another, an armoury; in another, a money-making factory (as we shall see presently). And yet, amid all this hubbub, were also queens and kings and nobles and children, all of them incarcerated, but all of them nonetheless somehow lived vividly. So the puzzles in this section will feature that flavour of their writings, and their communications with the outside world, some of which were secret, and some of which were coded, but all of which now pulsate with their own historical fascination. This was a world of trans-continental diplomacy, as well as intense religious revolution.

1

WORD PLAY

In the paragraph below, some words are missing. The missing words are all made up of the letters in THE TOWER OF LONDON. Can you play around with the words and fill the gaps just using those letters as many times as they appear in THE TOWER OF LONDON. For example, you can use a W only once in a word but you could use an O four times.

_ _ _ _ _ _ _ _ warders were looking for _ _ _ escaped _ _ _ _ _ _ but _ _ was _ _ _ _ _ _ _ to be seen. _ _ _ _ _ _ was _ _? Had _ _ _ _ _ _ _ _ them this time? _ _ had a secret _ _ _ _ _ _ for _ _ _ heir to the _ _ _ _ _ _ _, and if its secrets _ _ _ _ revealed they all could be in danger. Had _ _ already _ _ _ _ _ _ it away or buried it in a _ _ _ _ _ _ bed? _ _ _ _ _ _ _ _ _ warders, Thomas, Richard and Henry began to _ _ _ _ _ _ if the _ _ _ _ _ _ criminal was hiding _ _ _ _ near _ _ _ _ _ Green. Surely it was _ _ _ _ _ another look!

2

IN DISGUISE

Throughout the centuries, various forms of disguise have been used to get into, or get out of, the Tower. Here we have a disguise of a different kind. The 'clue' is disguised as a different word, using exactly the same letters in each case, in other words an anagram. See beyond the disguise and see that all is in order by completing the grid where words interlock.

ACROSS

7 Search

8 Co-Heir

10 Senator

11 Spare

12 Ache

13 Nerve

17 Frost

18 Reef

22 Parts

23 Engrave

24 Galore

25 Addles

DOWN

1 Tablets

2 Creches

3 Abets

4 Defeats

5 Wrote

6 Cares

9 Lancaster

14 Mentors

15 Gyrated

16 Dreamer

19 Gates

20 Roman

21 Large

3

OUT OF THE SHADOWS

The Tower has become notorious due to its reputation for executions over the years. In this puzzle we ask you to find the name of a famous person who died at the hands of an executioner, and also their final words at the scaffold.

Answer the questions, writing the answers horizontally in the upper grid, and the name of the person will appear reading down. When you have done this, take the shaded letters and write them vertically in the lower grid. Then, the ending of a quotation will be revealed horizontally.

1 Extreme greed to acquire money or power (7)

2 Without a pause, incessantly (3,4)

3 Bow the head to say yes (3)

   Attempt (3)

4 A long letter, usually a serious one (7)

5 An apiary, a home for honey-making insects (7)

6 Describes cultivation without using artificial pesticides (7)

7 A young hare (7)

8 Threw out forcibly (7)

9 Tree often found in churchyards (3)

   Tree which produces acorns (3)

10 Pure, unspoiled (7)

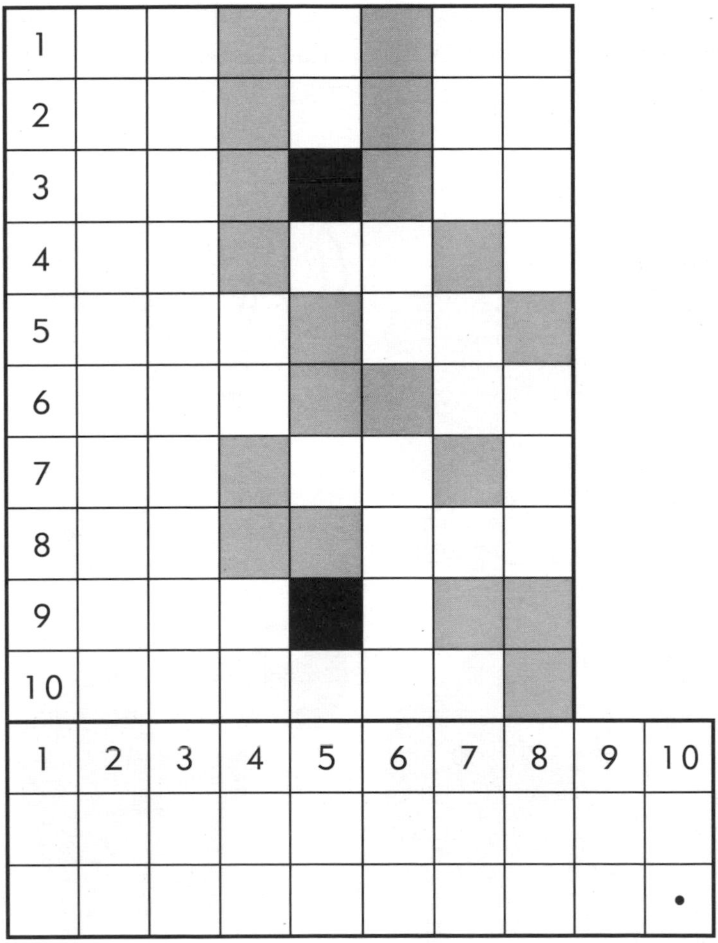
1
2
3
4
5
6
7
8
9
10
1 2 3 4 5 6 7 8 9 10

4

SINISTER SILHOUETTES

For many centuries, the doomed souls who met their fate by the axeman have been frequently seen in and around the Tower, none more so than in the Tudor period. Look at the three sinister silhouettes and decide which one – if any – of A, B or C matches the figure top right.

5

GUARD DUTY

Four guards are on duty in the Tower dungeons with its maze of corridors and passageways. The guards, Arthur, Bernard, Charles and Duncan, are each responsible for a prisoner with the same initial as himself; Lord Andover, Lord Beauchamp, Lord Crispin and Lord Douglas. The guards must not meet as they go and check on their charges and their paths must not cross. Can you plot out their lines of duty?

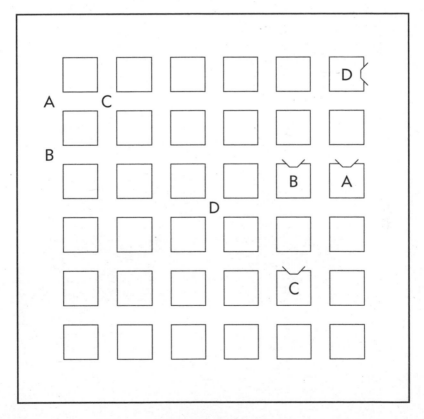

⌄⌄ DOORS OPEN THIS WAY

6

BROKEN BONES

Sadly, many sets of bones have been discovered throughout the ages at the Tower. In 1674, two skeletons were found which might have been the remains of the Princes in the Tower.

In the puzzles below, eight 'bones' have been broken into three parts, each part containing a three letter word. Put the twenty-four pieces back together so that they make eight, nine letter words.

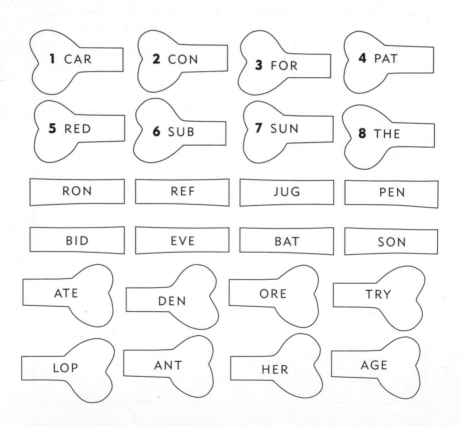

7

VOWEL PLAY

Vowel play certainly plays a part in this puzzle. Many famous people have been imprisoned at the Tower and some even met their end there. The names of high-profile prisoners listed below have had the consonants in their names removed so only the vowels remain. Can you work out who they were?

1 _ _ O _ A _   _ O _ E

2 A _ _ E   _ O _ E _ _

3 _ A _ _ E _ I _ E   _ O _ A _ _

4 _ _ O _ A _   _ U _ _ E _ _ E _

5 _ A _ _   _ A _ E   _ _ E _

6 _ _ O _ A _   _ _ O _ _ E _ _

7 _ I _   _ A _ _ E _   _ A _ E I _ _

8 _ U _   _ A _ _ E _

CHAPTER SIX

MAKING A MINT

Golden coins existed long before the Tower was built, but it was within the Tower that the business of making these coins for the realm was first gathered under one royal roof. It became, quite literally, a sweatshop industry.

In 1279, during the reign of Edward I, there was strong royal control over the making of money. This was a period when trade was increasing, and the phenomenon of forgery was also on the rise. As a growing fortress, the Tower made an ideal location for the secure workshops that would be needed. Indeed, it was so ideal that, for the next few centuries, coin-making was core to the Tower's activities. It even ended up benefitting from having one of the greatest scientists who ever lived join the staff.

So the puzzles in this section will have a distinctly financial flavour, from the elaborate designs of new coins to the ability to spot forgeries; from the grinding and searing technology needed to melt the metal, and then to form it anew into a token of value, to the mathematical headscratchers that royal treasuries can be prone to.

The Tower was not the first mint in London. The Romans had got there first, and their golden coins circulated through the land some thousand years before the Tower first came into existence. Then, once the Anglo Saxons had brought the kingdom together again, they too had their own system, with mints operating around the country. The silver penny of Alfred the Great featured a moulding of the king's head on one side, and a stylised monogram rendition of the word 'London' on the other. (An incredibly rare Alfred penny is available to see now in The Royal Mint Experience museum, Llantrisant, near Cardiff. For details, go to www.royalmint.com)

But the Norman Conquest of 1066, and the re-ordering of the land under its new aristocracy, came with a fast-developing new way of doing business. In 1279, William de Turnemire was given the role of 'Master Moneyer' of all England. The groat – that most redoubtable of medieval coins, still greatly valued in comedy sketches today – was first minted that same year.

Within the Tower of London, the coin factories were initially based not in sturdy chambers of stone, but in timber-built constructions around the walls. This gradually evolved as the Mint grew: a purpose-built area was put up in between the inner and outer walls of the fortress, in the north-west corner. It was named Mint Street.

From the start, those who worked there were scrutinised and searched carefully. There were still other mints around the country, but it was to the Tower that they all reported. The labour was intense and those who toiled there were endlessly faced with temptation, handling as they did valuable consignments of gold and silver, as well as brass and copper. In Mint Street there were ever-burning fires, and crucibles for melting the metals. They were then fashioned into thin sheets, and it was from these that the coins were pressed by hand.

There was no machinery for this in the Middle Ages and no protective clothing either, despite moving or pouring molten gold and silver and other metals being extraordinarily hazardous work. Hideous injuries were commonplace, as even the tiniest droplets seared and burned. Moreover, the air was thick with toxic chemicals, coating throats and lungs.

But there was art here, too. Engravers were sought to capture the likeness of each current monarch for use on the face of the coins. Once the engraving stamp was complete, the coins were produced by hand – each blank metal disc was placed beneath the stamp and hammered.

For some of those early medieval monarchs, the Mint offered temptations too rich to resist. In the 1280s, Edward I looked at all the silver being shipped into the Tower and thought: must this all be turned to currency? He found an alternative use for the expensive materials. A certain quantity was used to make beautiful silver utensils for his daughter. Added to this, the coinage that was produced was often diverted directly to the royal household, to pay for an array of fine fripperies.

Those violent Middle Ages also saw the Mint receiving raw materials from battlefield ransoms. Foreign powers would pay cash for prisoners and this, in turn, would be sent to the Mint, melted and repurposed into English money.

In the 1300s, the work at the Mint became even more intense, as a new form of coinage was introduced to give money more stability. Now there were ever more gold and silver coins, of higher values, than before. This meant that those working with the raw materials had to be both scrutinised constantly and trusted implicitly. Security and vigilance were tight, but there were apparently occasional instances when fragments of gold were swallowed by Mint workers, the intention being to retrieve them after their journey through the digestive system!

The gold was there because the old currency was losing its value. Merchants trading heavily with their European counterparts were wondering why it was not possible to use these European coins in England as well. England's response was to create gold coins that would demonstrate their superiority over the rest of Europe (nothing much changes!). Rather than have continental money in London, why not have glittering English currency in the bustling marketplaces of Paris and Ghent? These coins were intended to have a certain smartness and intricate delicacy of design, in order to show off the superiority of the Tower Mint.

The Mint was also at the centre of any national economic emergencies. The monarch (representing the nation) being short of money for use in raising armies for foreign wars would be a good example of a national economic emergency. One could not control the realm without controlling the production of money.

This was brought home rather sharply to King Charles I in the seventeenth century, during the English Civil War, when he was forced to flee London in 1642 and muster allies in different corners of the country, abandoning Mint Street to his foe, Oliver Cromwell. But there were other mints, at Aberystwyth in the west of Wales,

Shrewsbury and Oxford, which were especially busy throughout this period. For the Aberystwyth mint, Welsh silver was used. In Oxford, the engraver was Thomas Rawlins. And despite the tumult of the times, the coins issued by all these mints, down to the sixpences, were detailed and dignified. So much so, in fact, that they are particularly sought after by collectors today.

But, in the wake of the Civil War, and with the restoration of the monarchy following the Interregnum, a new spirit of scientific enquiry was burgeoning in Europe. The Tower of London and its Mint was to become the home of the man who revolutionised how the world was perceived, and who brought a wider understanding of the forces of the universe itself.

On the face of it, Isaac Newton was an unlikely candidate for the role of Warden of the Mint. Not only because, when younger, he had once inserted a thin dagger between his eyeball and eye-socket in order to prove that the resulting optical illusions of globes proved that the eyes did not always see objective reality (please, I implore you, do *not* try this at home). Not only because he had articulated gravity as a universal force, and thus changed the way the cosmos was seen. Not only because he was an anti-social academic at Cambridge, giving lectures on optics. But also because the job itself was regarded as a bit of flummery: a made-up occupation with a nice, fat guaranteed salary, promised to inner circles of friends.

The business of the Mint was now quite different to the infernal and primitive workshops of before. The diarist Samuel Pepys was taken on a tour of the newly mechanised mint in the late seventeenth century, and his eyes grew wide with admiration. Now there were mills, worked by donkeys, and better designed furnaces, moulds and rollers to keep production smooth. All of this had the effect of making the entire process more efficient. Pepys watched, mesmerised, as gold and silver was enclosed in lead, melted down, flattened and placed under special cutting frames to punch out the round coins and then pressed underneath a vast screw, the arms of which stretched out across the workshop.

By the time Isaac Newton moved into his new lodgings at the Tower – the official house of the Warden of the Mint – just a few years before the end of the seventeenth century, there was another dawning science in the land: economics. This was an increasingly globalised world. Not only was England steadily acquiring an empire, but the trade between London, Europe, and the farther corners of the world was intense. And at the centre of this new realm of hard cash was the Mint. It is often reckoned that currency crises had much more of an impact on everyday lives in those days than seemingly tumultuous events, such as the Glorious Revolution of 1688, in which the Dutch William of Orange grabbed the throne off his uncle (and father-in-law), James II. For most ordinary people at the time, there would actually have been little tangible difference whether they were ruled by James or William; by contrast, economic disasters touch every single corner of society.

One vast problem for the English currency was that its more valuable coins used silver; and this silver had more value in its pure state, when sold in Paris and other European cities. The result was that early bullion traders snapped up the coins and simply had them shipped out of the country to be melted down. Another huge problem was that of counterfeit money. There were rogues blessed with the artistic and technical skill to accurately replicate the likenesses and designs of coins. Additionally, there was the vexation of clipping – coins progressively losing their value because people were shaving off the valuable metal around the edges to melt down for their own purposes.

The Mint was central to the stability of the nation's economic well-being and so measures had to be taken. One surprisingly successful plan – initiated under the manically driven Isaac Newton – was to recall every last coin in the kingdom. The idea was that every single bit of money would be melted down, and recast, but with the valuable metals in each coin reduced and spread out over more coinage. Added to this, new technology meant novel means to thwart the counterfeiters, by making coins that had especially engraved edges, with grooves, so that any 'clipped' coins could be detected instantly.

The recall of the coins revealed the truth of the scale of counterfeiting: some twenty per cent of them were fake.

It might be thought that the man who had spent so long studying light prisms and the movement of the stars would have been other-worldly, divorced from grubby realities. But Isaac Newton applied himself to the Mint – and to the criminals who sought to undermine it – with the most extraordinary zeal. There was one especially prolific forger who would become Newton's chief nemesis: a career criminal called William Chaloner. Chaloner was sparky and inventive and lethally drawn to deception. For a while, he had set himself up in business as a doctor, or apothecary, and had a sideline on the streets of London selling marital aids imported from Italy, aimed at the female market. But he had also spent practically all of his adult life learning and refining new techniques for producing perfectly faked coins.

Cunning Chaloner developed an ingenious means, in parallel with Newton's ongoing innovations, of keeping the suspicious authorities off his back by a clever double bluff. He continually wrote to government and Mint officials, pretending to be a concerned citizen, an expert amateur, warning them of the new methods that the dastardly counterfeiters were using. Surely a man writing such letters could not himself be a forger? As such, he managed to take in a few prominent worthies in the Treasury, positioning himself as a trusted voice in the fight against crime. But Isaac Newton was having none of it.

Close to the Tower of London, in the claustrophobic little lanes of the City, there were a number of disreputable taverns; low-ceilinged establishments with dark nooks and decidedly mixed clientele. Newton set out to become an expert on the City's underworld and it was in such frowsy taverns that he carefully began cultivating contacts and informants, patiently hunting down his quarry. Sometimes Newton would even put on disguises to lurk in hostelries, watching and listening to get intelligence on the criminal networks. He was responsible for catching a number of other forgers. The charge was sometimes high treason; and the penalty was death.

In 1699, Chaloner was caught and arrested, and was faced with the shadow of the noose. In his increasing desperation, he tried to appeal to Isaac Newton. There are extraordinary letters in the National Archives, from Chaloner to the implacable Newton, clearly written in a state of terror. 'I shall be murdered unless you save me,' wrote Chaloner from his cell. 'Oh I hope God will move your heart with mercy and pity to do this thing for me.' Newton declined. Chaloner was hanged. And the Warden of the Mint continued stonily with his work.

Despite having such a tight grip on the nation's cash, and having piled up so much personal wealth from his Tower position, Newton's own savings were battered by the economic storm of the South Sea Bubble – a mad investment craze featuring the South Sea Company, which led to one of the first major financial crises, bringing bankruptcy and disaster not only to once-wealthy speculators but also potential ruin on a national scale. This proved that even the most rigorously scientific minds could fall prey to the irrational desires stoked by money. Within the precincts of the Tower, it was decreed that the words 'South Sea' should never be spoken within earshot of Isaac Newton.

The dawn of the Industrial Revolution at the end of the 1700s brought profound changes to the Royal Mint once again. Horses and donkeys turning mills were rendered redundant by steam. But there was scant room within the Tower's precincts for all the astonishing new machinery. Added to this, the ever-growing economy, in an ever more globalised trading world, meant that the Mint – which had started as a department of the Royal Household – was an integral part of the apparatus of a parliamentary government.

The moneyers did not move far, though, with new headquarters built just across the road, to the north-east of the Tower. These were opened for business in 1812. There they stayed (aside from temporary moves to locations such as Pinewood during the bombings of the Second World War) until 1966, at which point it became clear that the world – and demand – had moved on again and so, for the new decimal age, the Mint was moved to Wales, just outside Cardiff.

1

COINING IT

Thomas Slyboots was a well-known rogue who lived near the River Thames close by the Tower.

He went to a waterside tavern and issued a challenge to the innkeeper. 'I want to spend twenty-four coins on ale.' Thomas jangled the coins in a cloth bag. 'If you give me the amount of coins that I have in this bag, then I will spend twenty-four coins on your finest ale, and drinks all round.' The innkeeper was taken aback by Thomas's unusual challenge, and agreed to it. He counted out the coins in Thomas's bag, and gave him the same amount as agreed. Thomas counted out coins and slid them to the innkeeper, carefully putting the remaining coins in the cloth bag.

Some while later, Thomas rather unsteadily made his way to the butcher's. Thomas made the same suggestion to the butcher, who accepted the challenge. Thomas's coins were counted, the butcher gave him the same amount as agreed, then Thomas bought meat to the value of twenty-four coins.

Thinking his luck was too good to last, Thomas went to see a grain merchant. 'If you give me the amount of coins that I have in this bag, then I will spend twenty-four coins on sacks of grain.' Again, the coins were counted, the grain merchant then counted out the same number of coins from his pocket and gave them to Thomas. The rogue then took twenty-four coins, paid the merchant and went away with a sack of grain.

That was it for the day as Thomas's cloth bag was now completely empty.

How many coins did he have before he went into the tavern?

2

PENNY WISE

On the final day of the last century, four friends met up at a New Year's Eve party. They were all saying that it would be a good idea if they could save money on a regular basis. Bill recalled that his mother used to put loose change into a jar on the sideboard and would only spend the money on a special occasion. Andrea, Charles and Daisy all agreed they should try and follow a similar scheme.

The rules for their saving scheme were straightforward:

A penny was to be put in the pot on day one of the New Year. Two pennies would be saved on day two, three pennies on day three, four pennies on day four, and so on.

Twenty years slipped by before the four friends were reunited at a New Year's Eve party on 31 December 2019. They remember the scheme they talked about. What became of it?

Andrea confessed that she only saved for the first week then get bored. Bill saved until the end of January and then stopped. Charles kept going for three full months before accidentally breaking the pot. Thrifty Daisy actually kept saving for a whole year.

How many coins did each person save?

3

HEADS OR TAILS?

For many years, coins have shown a monarch's head on one side with a symbolic pattern on the other side. Throwing a coin in the air to see whether it lands showing HEADS or TAILS has settled many an argument.

We give you a total of ten definitions listed at random. Five words begin with HEAD. Five words end with TAIL. Can you toss a coin and solve the puzzle?

1   A drink made up of different fruit juices and spirits

2   Sale of goods to the public

3   Approach an employee of a different company

4   Small part of a painting, shown on its own

5   Clearance between the top of a vehicle and the underside of a bridge

6   Title of an article in a newspaper

7   Curb, cut short

8   Involve unavoidably

9   Self-willed or obstinate

10   Administrative centre of an organisation

4

POINTER

Here are ten coins on show on a table forming a triangle that points to the south.

Using the same ten coins and keeping them all on show, what is the least number of moves to form a triangle shape that points to the north?

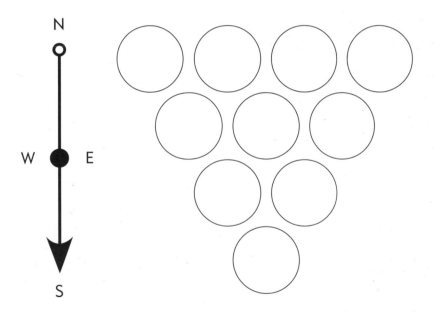

5

COIN COLLECTION

A new Mint worker has a pile of coins on his bench. He has been told by the Mint Warden that he must sort them into equal piles and there must be none left over. He is keen to make a good impression so he sets to work. He knows that there are no more than five hundred coins in front of him, and equally knows that there are at least fifty coins.

He sorts them into groups of three and there is one left over.

He sorts them into groups of four and there is one left over.

He sorts them into groups of five and there is one left over.

He sorts them into groups of six and there is one left over.

He sorts them into groups of seven and no coins are left over.

How many coins were on his bench at the beginning?

6

MINT STREET

Take a stroll down Mint Street within the Tower walls and identify the names or nicknames of coins down the ages from the quick-fire cryptic clues.

1 Monarch

2 Short hairstyle

3 Crush or beat

4 African country

5 Diminutive of a girl's name

6 Worker in leather

7 Headdress

8 Headdress broken in two

7

SPOT THE FAKES

Coin forgery was once considered to be treason with the death penalty or transportation for those found guilty. Look carefully at the eight coins below. They should all be identical. The majority of these coins are the same but some fake coins have been minted. How many fakes are on show?

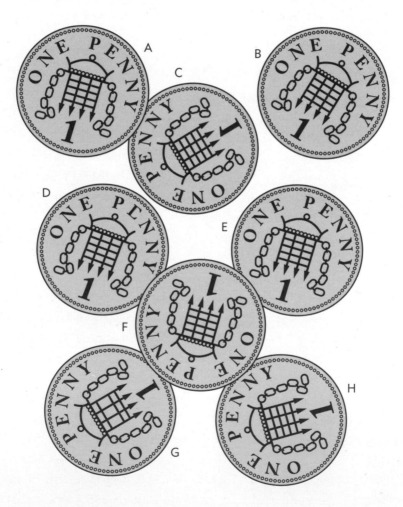

CHAPTER SEVEN

THE WIZARD AND THE SCHOOL OF NIGHT

EVEN in the early 1600s, the Tower was a tourist attraction. The main draw for the crowds at that time was the near-mythic figure of Sir Walter Raleigh.

On summer mornings, this buccaneer, pirate and polymath would stalk the battlements of the Tower, and rougher Londoners in the streets below would jostle for a glimpse of this proud, strutting personage, who would bow before his adoring fans. By that point, the once court favourite Sir Walter was prisoner within those walls. He was one of the many spies, intriguers and proto-terrorists incarcerated during that period, along with any others whom James I, the current monarch, considered dangerous.

In certain cases, James was right to be nervous. Sir Walter and some of his other illustrious companions in that Tower – by no means all prisoners – were men who thought all too freely, and whose intellects inquired into the darker corners of science and philosophy. This was a period when the Tower almost became a university; but a university for men whose ideas were sometimes considered too godless for the general public to bear. In the shadow of the White Tower, they founded a laboratory for experiments into the very heart of nature.

So, the puzzles in this section will be inspired by that early blend of weird alchemy and mathematics; by the immense scholarship that took place within the Tower that conjoined strange glass tubes and curious herbal and botanical mixtures. There will also be puzzles inspired by the Gunpowder Plot, and by the cunning riddles laid out by Sir Walter Raleigh in the metaphysical poetry that he wrote during this period.

Sir Walter was no stranger to the Tower. Across his long, fantastical career, he had been both a guard and a prisoner. When younger, he had been Captain of the Yeoman of the Guard. And he was present at one particularly extraordinary historical moment. Robert Devereux, the Earl of Essex, a former favourite of Elizabeth I, had fallen so far from grace that he had quite irrationally attempted an uprising against the monarch. Naturally, his messages were intercepted by the queen's secret service and the earl's final destination was the Tower (indeed, today's Devereux Tower is so named because that was the place in which he was held).

When the morning of his execution came, in the precincts of the Tower (it was considered too risky to carry out the beheading outside the walls, for fear of stirring an ugly riot among the earl's admirers), Sir Walter Raleigh was there with his Yeoman of the Guard, keeping a careful watch upon the proceedings. Raleigh was an old and bitter enemy of Essex. It was an enmity sparked partly by jealousy, as they had vied with each other for the queen's favour. And so, just before Essex made himself ready for the axeman, it was communicated to Raleigh that it might be better if he withdrew from the scene, for any sign of his gloating might provoke tumultuous scenes within the Tower walls as well. Sir Walter withdrew to the bulk of the White Tower as his rival was put to death with horrific clumsiness – the axeman slipped on his first try and hit Essex's shoulder instead.

The irony, though, was that Raleigh later succeeded in becoming a favourite of the queen, yet also failed to exercise caution. He had attained fame – and royal affection – for his exploits, including voyages to America, bringing back the potato and tobacco to England and founding a colony on Roanoake Island, which came to be called 'Virginia' in tribute to Queen Elizabeth. He was also a great help in suppressing an uprising in Ireland. That immortal and probably apocryphal legend of Sir Walter throwing his cloak across a puddle for his queen persists, but he certainly was willing to do a lot for her. He was also a serious poet and devoted works to Her Majesty, who had appeared therein as Cynthia, goddess of the moon.

But his downfall came when he secretly married one of Elizabeth's ladies-in-waiting. Somehow, he and his new wife thought they might succeed in keeping it quiet. Indeed, Bess Throckmorton was so intensely discreet for so long that even the birth of their child, Damerei, was kept from her mistress. Yet such news could hardly remain concealed for ever.

As a general rule, it was not just private passion or jealousy that led the queen to demand complete control over the emotional lives and relationships of her courtiers. It was also canny politics; love matches between sons and daughters of powerful families would have created new and influential dynasties. By demanding full knowledge, the queen was protecting her throne.

So this double betrayal from the handsome man that she so admired inspired a furious reaction. Not only Sir Walter, but his wife and their small baby, were consigned to the Tower in 1592. Husband and wife were not even permitted to occupy the same cell.

During their imprisonment there was an outbreak of plague; it insinuated itself through the fortress walls and the little baby died shortly afterwards. Bess Throckmorton was helpless with grief and the queen, now relenting with some pity and sympathy, had her released. A few weeks afterwards, Sir Walter himself was freed. But there was a bitter price to pay, as he found himself exiled from the royal court. This banishment in some ways hurt more than the Tower incarceration. He set about writing an epic series of metaphysical poems for the queen – in essence, beautiful cryptograms that were intent upon winning back her precious favour. They did not.

The accession to the throne of James I (James VI of Scotland) brought yet more tribulations for Sir Walter, when he was suspected of conspiring with others against this new reign. This was 'The Main Plot', and would have involved placing Lady Arbella Stuart on the throne. The chief plotters were indeed acquaintances of Sir Walter's, but there was no hard evidence that showed him having any real involvement with their whispered plans.

Nonetheless, there was a number of people at court who disliked Raleigh vehemently enough to influence King James's opinion. The plotters – and Sir Walter – were sentenced to death. In Sir Walter's case, though, the sentence was commuted to life imprisonment within the Tower.

To begin with, the sentence weighed exceedingly heavily upon Sir Walter. The Lieutenant of the Tower, Sir John Peyton, in whose charge he now reposed, observed of his prisoner: 'I never saw so strange a dejected mind as in Sir Walter Raleigh. I am exceedingly cumbered [burdened] with him; five or six times a day he sendeth for me in such passions as I see his fortitude is impotent to support his grief.'

The one-time buccaneer was no longer safe around knives, having threatened to take his own life. All his estate and financial affairs he had turned over to his beloved wife. But even the darkest winter must give way to spring. And – as with Thomas More and Lady Jane Grey before him – there seemed to be something about the fortress that somehow, eventually, brought out a renewed energy and intellectual appetite. He was simply too much of a polymath, too interested in the workings of the world around him, not to rise once more out of these depths.

Perhaps one of the factors in Sir Walter's irrepressible energy was that he was not imprisoned within a cell, but in the upper floor of the Bloody Tower. There are many even now who would regard this as a rather pleasant *pied à terre*. Raleigh's chamber overlooked the tranquil prospect of the Lieutenant's garden. It had a fireplace, table, chairs, space for books, light for study. Upon his initial arrival, when he was convinced that he would be facing the executioner, Raleigh had written to his wife Bess. In the tenderest terms, he urged her not to waste all her time in grief and that death was to put them asunder, and so she ought to marry again. This he urged not only for her sake but for the sake of their second child – also called Walter.

As it turned out, there was no need. And although Sir Walter was confined within the walls of the fortress, he was allowed family visits, and servants to attend him. And so Bess remained devoted to him. They were also blessed with a third child, whom they named Carew. He was not only conceived within the Tower but, as rumour has it, was born there too.

The garden beneath Sir Walter's window became part of the new pattern of his life. His fascination with horticulture had extended far beyond the exotic imports that he had brought back from the Americas. The Lieutenant of the Tower decided to allow Sir Walter use of a section of the garden for the cultivation of herbs, perhaps happy not to be 'cumbered with his passions' any more.

Many of these herbs, used in elaborate mixtures, were intended to be medicinal. He formulated a recipe for strawberry water, involving the fruit steeped in pure spirits, before being strained, and then mixed with pure water. This was merely a pick-me-up. Sir Walter also concocted what he termed the 'Great Cordial', intended to cure and alleviate a wide variety of ills. Among some of the more common garden herbs to be found in this elixir were certain more hard-to-come-by ingredients, such as deer's horn, powder from pearls and a substance that could only be acquired with some difficulty by ocean-going sailors: ambergris. This was an oil found in the intestinal systems of sperm whales. Then there was the addition of viper's flesh, and the internal organs of other snakes too. All seasoned with cinnamon, nutmeg, saffron and cloves. All of the above were transformed into a thick syrup, which was then burned, reduced to a sort of ashy mulch, and then added to sugary water. Raleigh had no doubts about its efficacy, and indeed the recipe and the ingredients were studied for many years to come. (Possibly one beneficial effect might have been the sense of relief that came when one had stopped drinking it.)

King James's wife, Anne, however, was a great believer in the powers of this particular medicine, and when their son, Prince Henry, was stricken with typhoid, she administered it in terrible hope. Naturally it was no cure, and when the prince died, Raleigh was stricken. Not least because the young man had been a particular supporter, who once marvelled that his father should, as he put it, keep such a bird locked up in a cage.

Raleigh's wife Bess was as keen a gardener as her husband and they worked together in the shaded parts of the Tower precincts, where they had an old hen shed converted for Raleigh's more delicate specimens. Other medicines of his own devising were eagerly sought after from afar. The wife of the French ambassador, for instance, was particularly keen on his 'Balsam of Guiana'. This slightly more appetising-sounding refreshment was composed of borage and rosemary, marigold and dark red carnation flowers, mixed with juniper and saffron and blended with syrup of roses and lemon juice. It was said to be particularly effective for women who had recently given birth, as a strength-giving tonic.

The secret garden must have been a psychic balm for Sir Walter, and, indeed, so was his writing. Again, despite his status as prisoner, he was allowed to keep and borrow any number of books, and his studies were prodigious. As well as the labyrinthine conceits of his metaphysical poetry, there was also his tremendous appetite for history. It was while confined to this small realm that he embarked upon the first volume of his *Historie of The World*, starting with Creation and ending at about 100 BC. This book would later turn out to be a huge popular hit, despite remaining unfinished.

King James initially sought to suppress this work for being 'too saucy in censuring Princes' – in other words, too critical of God-given authority – but, by 1614, it appeared on the bookstalls, and it seems to have been the very prototype of a bestseller.

And so we might imagine Raleigh in his Tower apartments: his study on the ground floor of the Bloody Tower, with two windows admitting the daylight; the chambers above, reached by a narrow stone spiral staircase, where he and sometimes his wife and children would live and sleep; the fuggy fireplaces, the upstairs door out on to the battlements, which overlooked on one side the White Tower and on the other, the river. How often did he gaze upon that water and dream? And then, in 1616, the unexpected chance to embark once more upon the oceans came, when Raleigh was pardoned and released to lead an expedition to Guiana, in search of the legendary golden city of El Dorado.

For such a fearsome buccaneer, Raleigh was, by some accounts, a terrible sailor: prone to seasickness, and apparently almost completely unable to sleep when the ship encountered rough weather. The expedition was an agonising disaster, in which Raleigh lost one of his sons in a battle with the Spanish at an outpost, and it ended in him and his remaining unslaughtered crew being forced to limp back to England.

There was now no more time left for this most unusual and mercurial of courtiers. His earlier pardon was on condition that neither he nor his crews could launch attacks on Spanish outposts. And now the outraged Spanish ambassador in London demanded his execution. King James assented. Sir Walter was at last sentenced to the death that he had evaded fifteen years previously. He was removed from the Tower and taken to Westminster. Before the axe was brought down, he was alleged to have eyed it and observed: ''Tis a sharp remedy, but a sure one for all ills.' His loving wife Bess was permitted to retrieve and keep his head, which had been preserved.

With Raleigh's death, a fascinating intellectual light had been extinguished, but a fellow trailblazer at the Tower lived on. One of his more extraordinary co-prisoners for so many years was the ninth Earl of Northumberland, Henry Percy, who was nicknamed 'the Wizard Earl'.

He had been thrown in the Tower in 1605 on suspicion of involvement with the Gunpowder Plot. But there were also suggestions that King James was frightened of the forty-year-old earl because of his interest in sorcery. In actual fact, Henry Percy was interested in forbidden knowledge that was rather more powerful than mere magic, and his time at the Tower was alive with the fireworks of scientific discovery. In his rooms he had over five hundred volumes, an astounding library. Servants travelled to and fro from his grand palace at Syon Park, collecting yet more scholarly material for their master.

The hugely wealthy earl had had a rackety youth in which, he confessed, his chief interests were 'hawks, hounds, horses, dice, cards, apparel, mistresses'. But there was, from an early age, much more to him than that. He and Raleigh went back a long way. Both men had a long-standing fascination with mathematics and philosophy, astronomy and alchemy. It was whispered that they both also had an interest in the occult. The earl earned the nickname 'Wizard' because he was perceived by ignorant peers to be dabbling in the shadowy arts. He and Raleigh – and possibly the playwright Christopher Marlowe – had belonged to a rumoured society called The School of Night.

A rich subject for wide-eyed gossip, The School of Night was imagined to be a hotbed of forbidden atheism; of young men saying out loud what others would hardly dare to think for fear of death and eternal damnation. Whatever the truth of this society, it is certainly the case that Raleigh and Henry Percy were like minds and their dual incarceration in the Tower – together with their privileges in hosting visitors – meant that, for a while, the Tower of London became an intellectual hothouse.

Between them, the Wizard Earl and the great buccaneer managed to draw some of the greatest and most incisive minds of the age, and the Tower soon became a base for a range of new scientific experiments. As well as leading and pioneering mathematicians, such as Walter Warner and Thomas Hughes, there were regular visits from the rumoured leading light of The School of Night: a scientist called Thomas Harriot, who had dealings with Queen Elizabeth's astrologer, Dr Dee. Harriot was passionately interested in astronomy and was the first man to have used a telescope to make sketches of the moon.

To trailblaze in science at that particular point of history was still fraught with danger, as accusations of atheism could then lead to darker judgements of black magic. For those who could not grasp the import of scientific enquiries into gravity and starlight and chemistry, Harriot and the rumoured School of Night were dabbling in matters that were better left to the Creator.

And Harriot had himself been imprisoned in the Tower, briefly, in the wake of the Gunpowder Plot, when he was suspected of having cast a horoscope to show when the stars would predict the downfall of King James. As mentioned, James was especially susceptible to fear of the supernatural.

After his release from the Tower, Thomas Harriot actually moved back in voluntarily, in order to marshal the earl's converted furnace (adjacent to Sir Walter Raleigh's herbarium), with its glass tubes and alchemy laboratory. The Wizard Earl was, by then, paying Harriot's pension, or salary, and had provided him with a house near his own riverside stately palace. Among their diverse fields of enquiry were the trajectory of cannonballs, the optics of rainbows, and even the possibilities of movement and flight outside of the earth's orbit. In an era when it was not widely understood that the earth moved around the sun, it is little wonder then that some considered Harriot a magician.

The more elegant elements of London society were eager to attend the informal court of Raleigh and the Wizard Earl. Sometimes there were complaints at the Tower gates about the crush of smart horse-drawn coaches, queuing impatiently, their aristocratic occupants awaiting their opportunity to pay visits. Here was the last flame of the Renaissance, the dazzling minds whose taste for knowledge had in so many ways transformed the face of the country.

Yet, juxtaposed in the Tower with the light of intellectual endeavour was the darkness of its prisons, and the barbaric horrors that lay within for less exalted captives. The Gunpowder Plot of 1605 was an historical moment that, in some ways, was a turning point for the Tower itself.

Guy or Guido Fawkes had converted to Catholicism as a young man, having been brought up a Protestant. In his zeal, he sailed away from England to Spain, in order to join the Catholic war against the Protestant Dutch. Fawkes's life changed definitively when, still in Spain, he met another English Catholic fighting for the cause. Thomas Winter was the cousin of one Robert Catesby, who, back in England, was plotting a coup. A coup for which courageous volunteers would be required.

The conspirators met at a riverside house in Lambeth. Of all of them, Fawkes was the one with the technical expertise, as he had learned how to correctly handle gunpowder in Spain. These men placed barrels of gunpowder in the cellars of the Palace of Westminster, ready to be detonated at the State Opening of Parliament. Of course, as we all remember each fifth of November, the plot was discovered. Fawkes was first brought before King James, where he boldly told the king that it had been his intention to 'blow' him and all other Scottish lords 'back to Scotland'.

Thence he was sent to the Tower, and to his terrible interrogation in the musty cellars that lay beneath the White Tower. He withstood the rack, amid other tortures, for an excruciating several days before finally giving way and naming co-conspirators. Fawkes's shaky, post-interrogation signature might be one of the most gruesomely famous in history. Fawkes, along with Thomas Winter and several other surviving conspirators (the others were shot dead while being pursued), was imprisoned for a time within the Tower. And then, with hideous ceremony, they were hauled through the streets to Westminster, where they were hanged, drawn and quartered. In terms of the Tower, this was one of the last occasions when it was used specifically for the nightmarish torture of prisoners. Even by 1605, instruments such as the rack were being viewed by many as machines more fitting to an uglier, more barbaric age.

Therefore, the puzzles in this section will not dwell so much on gory ordeal, but rather upon the extraordinary, amazing minds who were gathered within those walls in that period; a cornucopia of fiendish enigmas befitting a celebration of mathematics and a new era of logical deduction. The time when the Tower of London was an ivory tower of learning and scientific discovery.

1

THE CANNONBALL CONUNDRUMS

DURING the time that Sir Walter Raleigh was held prisoner in the Tower, he had many fascinating discussions with the pioneering mathematician and astronomer Thomas Harriot. As well as having innovative ideas about the use of algebra, Harriot was gripped by immediate and practical problems. And as both he and Sir Walter Raleigh had voyaged extensively across the world's oceans, some of these problems were directly related to life on deck. There was of course the perennial challenge of navigation to overcome, as longitude was yet to be discovered. Then there were the smaller but no less perplexing issues, such as The Cannonball Problem.

In itself, it seemed perfectly simple: how best to stack a number of cannonballs so that the space on deck is used most sparingly and efficiently?

Curiously, though, the question set in train some marvellous mathematical insights on the part of Harriot. Down through the centuries, subsequent complex equations concerning the properties of spheres, squares and pyramids from other mathematicians proved those insights, and indeed, the problem is still discussed today as a wonderful example of the use of three-dimensional reasoning in maths problems.

To make life a little more straightforward – after all, not all of us are dab hands with quadratic equations – here are some mental challenges involving all those loose cannonballs on the deck.

CANNONBALL CONUNDRUM 1:

There are fifty-five cannonballs. It is best to stack them in the shape of a pyramid. This being the case – the cannonballs built up layer upon layer – how many cannonballs will form the bottom layer?

CANNONBALL CONUNDRUM 2:

For ease of reaching, smaller piles of cannonballs are kept ready by the cannons on the ship's deck. There are whole mathematical theories devoted to the shape of piles such as these, and of how the space might be utilised even more efficiently. But here's a question for you:

There are ten cannonballs in each pile. How many cannonballs are to be counted in each bottom layer?

CANNONBALL CONUNDRUM 3:

Thomas Harriot's reasoning with the cannonballs resonates today, and often in the most down-to-earth ways. One of which is to do with exports and freight; if one is selling something cube-shaped, like Rubik's famous puzzle toy, for instance, then it can be packed with perfect efficiency. But if the objects for sale are spherical or round – oranges, for instance – then in a rectangular packing space, there will inevitably be spaces between them. Across the years, mathematicians have looked at formulas to try and make the best use of space, all sparked by Harriot in the sixteenth century, and now it is time for you to have a go.

If you were to transport twenty-four flat, perfectly round discs, and put each one into an individual frame so that they would be packed closely together – what shape frame would minimise all the spaces between the discs?

2

THE CHALLENGE OF TRAJECTORY

In many senses a visionary, Thomas Harriot delved deep into a wide range of problems that were then mysterious phenomena, from the optics of rainbows and the paradoxes of light refraction, to the landscape of the moon as seen through his telescopes. This is why his patron the Earl of Northumberland, prisoner and neighbour of Sir Walter Raleigh in the Tower, found him so endlessly stimulating.

Harriot was also gripped by the practical geometry of warfare, in particular the mathematics of trajectory. If one were to fire a cannonball, how could you calculate not only the distance it flies, but also the shape its flight makes in the sky? He was the first to come very close to calculating a mathematical formula in order to find an optimum angle for cannonballs to be fired from.

But the question for you – for which no maths knowledge whatsoever is needed – is this:

Even though Harriot came very close to working out the shape of the arc that a cannonball or a similar heavy projectile might make in the sky, he was flummoxed by one element that would always have produced the incorrect answer. There was one crucial aspect of gravity that neither he – nor indeed anyone else – had quite grasped by the early 1600s.

Imagine for yourself that cannonball flying through the air, in contrast say to a simple arrow – what are the key factors that influence the rate of descent of both an arrow and cannonball? And what was the one thing that Harriot could not believe?

3

THE RIDDLES OF THE TOWER

In addition to all his other dazzling talents, Sir Walter Raleigh was a gifted poet. In the Elizabethan period, such an aptitude was considered very becoming of a gentleman. He was not the only Tower of London prisoner to have a gift for verse. Sometime before him, during Henry VIII's reign, Thomas Wyatt – an ambassador, pioneering poet and rumoured lover of Anne Boleyn – was held captive there, in considerably less comfortable circumstances. One feature of Elizabethan literature and culture was a taste for puzzles and riddles, and indeed, both of the gentlemen above sprinkled their sonnets with teasing enigmas. These were poems akin to today's cryptic crosswords, but much more aesthetically pleasing. Below are two such poems from Sir Walter Raleigh and two from Thomas Wyatt.

Across the great gulf of years, can you now discern their hidden messages?

POEM 1:

'Sir Walter Raleigh to His Son'

Three things there be that prosper up apace,
And flourish while they grow asunder far;
But on a day, they meet all in a place,
And when they meet, they one another mar.

And they be these: the Wood, the Weed, the Wag:
The Wood is that that makes the gallows tree;
The Weed is that that strings the hangman's bag;
The Wag, my pretty knave, betokens thee.

Now mark, dear boy, while these assemble not,
Green springs the tree, hemp grows, the wag is wild;

But when they meet, it makes the timber rot,
It frets the halter, and it chokes the child.

God bless the child!

By Sir Walter Raleigh

So, what blackly humorous advice is the father imparting to his son?

POEM 2:

'On the Cards and Dice'

Before the sixth day of the next new year,
Strange wonders in this kingdom shall appear:
Four kings shall be assembled in this isle,
Where they shall keep great tumult for awhile.
Many men then shall have an end of crosses,
And many likewise shall sustain great losses;
Many that now full joyful are and glad,
Shall at that time be sorrowful and sad;
Full many a Christian's heart shall quake for fear,
The dreadful sound of *trump* when he shall hear.
Dead bones shall then be tumbled up and down,
In every city and in every town.
By day or night this tumult shall not cease,
Until an herald shall proclaim a peace;
An herald strange, the like was never born,
Whose very beard is flesh and mouth is horn.

By Sir Walter Raleigh

More black comedy: what is the 'tumult' that Sir Walter is describing? And what is this 'strange herald' that arrives to bring peace once more?

POEM 3:

What word is that that changeth not,
Though it be turned and made in twain?
It is mine answer, God it wot,
And eke the causer of my pain.
(It) love rewardeth with disdain:
Yet is it loved. What would ye more?
It is my health eke and my sore.

By Thomas Wyatt

So, what is this word that doesn't change no matter which way it is turned? The answer is said to have sinister historical significance, connected with Wyatt's romantic life . . .

POEM 4:

A lady gave me a gift she had not,
And I received her gift I took not.
She gave it me willingly and yet she would not,
And I received it albeit I could not.
If she gave it me I forced not,
And if she take it again she cares not.
Conster what this is, and tell not,
For I am fast sworn I may not.

By Thomas Wyatt

What then is this extraordinary gift that is neither given nor received?

4

THE REBELLIOUS CIPHERS

Many of the Tower's more illustrious prisoners were adept with codes and ciphers. We have seen how the Catholic John Gerard cunningly utilised orange juice to write secret messages to supporters. During the reigns of Elizabeth I and James I others employed slightly more sophisticated ciphers. In 1585, Elizabeth's great rival to the throne, Mary Queen of Scots, was under house arrest, and so her fervent followers had to write to her in code. One of the more famous of these followers was Anthony Babington, a gentleman in his mid-twenties. He was not to know that the Catholic circles around Mary had been infiltrated by the agents of Elizabeth's spymaster Francis Walsingham. And so, Babington's letters to Mary, rendered in cipher, were intercepted and their codes broken. Babington was taken to the Tower, and thence suffered the hideous fate of being hanged, drawn and quartered.

Here are two historic extracts from Babington's communications with Mary in 1585. They are not only declarations of support, but also signals of intent to assassinate Elizabeth I. The substitution code we have employed here is a shade more straightforward than the original, but the challenge remains: with just a couple of clues to the key, can you unravel the seditious messages?

Clues: Coded numbers and letters alternate. As with a mirror, think right to left.

One word to start: 'D J 13 D' is 'THAT'.

CRYPTIC CODE 1:

7 1 4 11 H K   2 9 D J   D 11 G   10 11 G D H 11 7 11 G
13 G L   13   J 3 G L E 11 L   6 K   6 3 E   K 6 H H 6 2 11 E 4
2 9 H H   3 G L 11 E D 13 8 11   D J 11   L 11 H 9 C 11 E 1
6 K   1 6 3 E   E 6 1 13 H   F 11 E 4 6 G   K E 6 7   D J 11
J 13 G L 4   6 K   1 6 3 E   11 G 11 7 9 11 4.

CRYPTIC CODE 2:

D J 11 E 11   M 11   4 9 B   G 6 M H 11
10 11 G D H 11 7 11 G,   13 H H   7 1   F E 9 C 13 D 11
K E 9 11 G L 4,   2 J 6   K 6 E   D J 11   A 11 13 H   D J 11 1
M 11 13 E   D 6   D J 11   12 13 D J 6 H 9 12
12 13 3 4 11   13 G L   1 6 3 E   7 13 1 11 4 D 1' 4
4 11 E C 9 12 11   2 9 H H   3 G L 11 E D 13 8 11
D J 13 D   D E 13 10 9 12 13 H   11 B 11 12 3 D 9 6 G.

CHAPTER EIGHT

ALL THAT GLITTERS

SOME rare jewels contain the depth of centuries. When you stare into their richly coloured hearts, you cannot help imagining all the history that unfolded around them. In the Tower of London, the Crown Jewels may be viewed by first stepping on to a slow-moving passenger conveyor belt, upon which you glide past the twinkling display of crowns and orbs. This is an elegant way to prevent you standing in the same spot for hours, ignoring the queues behind, as you become hypnotised not only by the spectacle, but by all the extraordinary stories that surround these bewitching stones.

The puzzles in this section are directly inspired by the Tower's jewel house, and the unfathomable treasures within. With conundrums involving not only the geometry of diamonds and the ability to see the fakes among the real things, but also nefarious brainteasers to do with planned heists and plots. The history of the Crown Jewels is not only about power and wealth, but about desire. And some of these extraordinary gems also have their legends and curses, as if such unearthly beauty must also have supernatural protection.

But, in addition to this, there are other parts of the story of the Crown Jewels that are startlingly contemporary. Many were only added to the collection in the last few centuries, and this is partly down to the revolutionary republican Oliver Cromwell, who had no time for the sensuous fripperies of royalty.

The first crown to become an essential part of the ceremonial continuity of the throne was the one which was worn by Edward the Confessor in the eleventh century. It was said to have been a circlet of gold, decorated with filigree patterns and set with just a few gems. The entire idea of a golden crown was one that had been imported from the East, it is thought. This symbol of royal authority, and the sceptre that the king also carried, were kept safe by the monks at Westminster Abbey. When the by then long dead Edward was made a saint in the twelfth century, his crown acquired ever more spiritual significance. There are accounts of St Edward's Crown being presented at the enthronement of Henry III, together with the tradition that, at the moment it was placed on the monarch's head, it had an extra kind of holy power.

In tapestries and medieval paintings, the succession of kings across the years that followed appear to be wearing the same crown; confirmation that the tradition was indeed passed down through the ages. But the Tudors made a few changes. A new version of St Edward's Crown was commissioned – either by Henry VII or Henry VIII – and this was a rather richer and more eye-catching model. Here was a crown with arches wrought of gold, engraved patterns of fleur-de-lis, and which was embedded with precious jewels. It held diamonds and rubies, wedded with the hypnotic blue of sapphires and the deep green of emeralds. There were pearls too, and a new use of religious imagery. Around the crown, on its engraved 'petals', were images of Christ, and Mary, and St George. It is thought that this was to give extra weight to Henry VIII's newfound authority over England's churches, following the break with Rome and the ensuing Reformation.

This later, Tudor crown recurs in the rather more detailed royal portraits that came with the Renaissance. And it was certainly passed on, through the reigns of Elizabeth and James I, to Charles I. But, in 1649, the monarchy was abolished. Charles was taken to the scaffold and executed. And the Lord Protector, Oliver Cromwell, made his iconoclastic decision that the crown, and all the other jewels and valuables that made up the royal collection, were either to be melted down for bullion or sold off. The plan received Parliamentary assent.

There were those under orders to melt the crown in the red-hot crucible in the Tower blacksmith's forge who felt a quiver of unease, however. After all, the crown carried religious as well as royal significance. And those who worked at the Tower of London's Jewel House were outraged and horrified. The clerk who kept the keys of the House – Carew Mildmay – protested, and refused to allow the Parliamentary officers in to seize the jewels. He was arrested, and placed behind bars. Diamonds, rubies and pearls were dug out of the regalia and the gold of the crown was turned into coins.

And all those fascinating, flashing jewels were scattered to the wider world, into the hands of rich collectors. But there was one in particular – a blood-red gem of extraordinary size and depth – that carried a huge amount of significance, and which was particularly sought after by a monarchist collector who wished to ensure that at least one part of a centuries-old custom was kept within the realm.

The jewel in question was known as the Black Prince's Ruby. The size of an egg, and possessing a mesmerising red depth, this gem was not in fact a ruby, but an even rarer and more valuable spinel. Its journey across the medieval world was epic and the fact that it is in the Tower of London today is an impressive tribute to the tenacity of tradition.

The Black Prince's Ruby was mined hundreds of years ago in the mountains of what is now Tajikistan. The jewel travelled with merchants along the Silk Road, across deserts and steppes, east to west, and, by the 1300s, it had been taken to what is now Spain, then a region of disparate kingdoms. Already famous for its hypnotic qualities, the spinel had come into the possession of Abu Said, the Moorish ruler of Granada. That was until Don Pedro of Seville, a rival warlord, launched an attack and Abu Said lost the day, and the beautiful jewel. But Don Pedro, in turn, came to face attack – notably, from his own brother – and he was forced to flee north to Bordeaux. There dwelt Edward of Woodstock, son of Edward III, who was otherwise known as the Black Prince. In 1366, Don Pedro sought sanctuary, and the Black Prince named his price. He wanted the fascinating jewel.

It was rumoured that the ruby was cursed, and would bring the downfall of anyone who possessed it. The Black Prince had, in his youth, found fame as an extraordinary military commander in the Hundred Years' War, and his name had become a by-word for knightly virtue and chivalric pursuits. Yet the wheel of fortune (an image favoured by the poet Chaucer) whirled violently and when the prince returned to England in 1371, the ruby closely protected, his life started to go into a dramatic decline. His health deteriorated, he contracted dysentery, and he soon knew that he was looking at the prospect of an early grave. He died so young, at just forty-six, that his father outlived him. Was all this down to the curse of the jewel?

Nonetheless, this was how the Black Prince's Ruby was transported to England, where it came to occupy a vital position amid the Crown Jewels. The prince's surviving son – the eldest had died – was the boy who would become Richard II. Did the ruby bring that tragic misfortune upon his reign, which ended with his cousin Bolingbroke deposing him and having him murdered – or left to starve – in a cell in Pontefract Castle?

The ruby then passed to Bolingbroke, now Henry IV, and his own reign was soon beset with woes, with civil strife and warring increasing, combined with the king's own ill-health.

In 1415, this extraordinary gem went on to acquire a near legendary status when a young, dashing King Henry V wore it upon his crown as he landed in France and made ready for what was to become known as the Battle of Agincourt. And, indeed, if there had been a curse, it must surely have been reversed. On the morning of the battle, Henry was arrayed in golden gilt armour, and the ruby – or spinel – was at the centre of a crown that was also festooned and flashing with pearls and sapphires. This was not merely a glittering display of wealth and power. According to legend, the Black Prince's Ruby actually helped to save Henry's life, when he was being set upon by several hacking swordsmen: the jewel absorbed what could have been a fatal gash to the head.

The ruby's malign reputation reasserted itself, however, when the brilliant Henry was struck down at the young age of thirty-five with fatal dysentery. And his heir, Henry VI, so retiring and modest and unsuited for the crown, met his own horribly unhappy end at the Tower of London, as we have seen in earlier chapters. His alleged murderer (at least, according to Shakespeare) inherited the crown and the ruby; much good that it did Richard III at Bosworth Field – when he was cut down in battle, apparently the Black Prince's Ruby rolled into the bloody mud, close to the slain monarch. According to the story, it was retrieved and solemnly handed on to the first Tudor King, Henry VII, and it was at this point that the jewel became an even more central part of the growing ceremonial regalia of the monarch, up to, and after, the shock of the Civil War and the Interregnum.

The identity of the spinel's mysterious buyer is lost in the mists of obscurity, but whoever that Cavalier benefactor was, the gem was kept safe until the throne was restored in 1660 and it was sold back (presumably at a handsome price) to the new monarch, Charles II. Almost two hundred years later, at the coronation of Queen Victoria in 1838, the glowing red spinel now formed the centrepiece of a new imperial crown that had been made for the new queen. A hundred years later again, and there was another redesigned crown, this time lighter, but still featuring the gem at its centre.

This is the crown we still see today, worn by the monarch at the State Opening of Parliament. And there is something poetic about the idea that, after so many centuries, the jewel still has the power to make onlookers at the Tower catch their breath as they stare into the heart of it.

The coronation crown itself, remade for Charles II in 1661 and most recently, in an updated form, placed upon the head of Her Majesty in Westminster Abbey in 1953, is one of those treasures that now looks so familiar that it is almost easy to take it for granted. It is famously heavy; its golden arches, surmounted by orb and cross, are said to put tremendous pressure on the neck. It was only comparatively recently, however, that the flashing inset jewels were a permanent feature; up until the twentieth century, the diamonds and sapphires and rubies would have been borrowed or hired for the coronation itself, and then returned. These days, the jewels are permanent.

At the coronation, the sovereign holds a golden orb, which is also surmounted with a jewelled cross. This object is intended to represent the world of Christian faith. There is also a golden sceptre that, as with the orb, dates back to the reign of Charles II. But the tradition stretches back into the darker past: by some accounts, it was a feature of William the Conqueror's coronation ceremony: 'By the sceptre, uprising in the kingdom are controlled, and the rod gathers and confines those men who stray.' But its most awesome feature is a startlingly recent addition. In 1910, the sceptre was reset so that its apex could be dominated by the world's largest cut white diamond. It was at the coronation of George V in 1910 that the Cullinan I diamond – then valued at around £40 million – became a permanent feature of the sceptre.

There is another jewel within the collection that has a fame which towers over that of even the Black Prince's Ruby. The Koh-i-Noor diamond has a story that spans continents and centuries of conquest, bloodshed and desire. It is difficult to say where in India, Pakistan or Afghanistan the vast white diamond was first found, but, by the 1500s, and the invasion of India by the Mughals, it already had its own fame.

It was placed at the head of what was known as the Peacock Throne of the Mughal rulers. That is, a throne shaped like the glorious fanned wings of the bird and inset with innumerable precious stones. According to some accounts, there was a preference in that period for stones of colour, and so the rich greens of emeralds and the mesmerising blues of sapphires were prized even higher than diamonds. But the Koh-i-Noor was a status symbol in a realm of its own. Its name, translated from Persian, means 'mountain of light', which was how one maharajah described its majestic brilliance.

By the 1700s, successive dynasties were rising and falling, and the measurelessly valuable diamond passed from one ruler to another. Ranjit Singh acquired it in the early 1800s and he soon became paranoid about guarding it while he wore it in public. The diamond was held in a pannier atop a camel, but there were two dozen other camels identically equipped, for security, should any thief think of attempting a robbery.

And by this time the rapacious British, whose commercial concerns had been swallowing India like a mighty snake, had their own vehement interest in acquiring the diamond. They had added the Kingdom of Punjab to their growing empire, and the Koh-i-Noor came with the territory. There was a contract that stated that it 'shall be surrendered by the Maharajah of Lahore to the Queen of England'. By now, it not only represented wealth, but ultimate power.

The voyage to England with the stone was fraught with hazard. There was an outbreak of cholera on board the ship and mighty storms sent it wildly off course. But, by 1850, the vast diamond was in England, and being presented to Queen Victoria at Buckingham Palace.

Prince Albert, Queen Victoria's husband, noted the disappointed responses from people who thought that the vast natural diamond might just be a lump of glass because of its lack of brightness and sent it away to be cut, in an act of desecration that surely would not be allowed today. Around half its surface was chiselled away in pursuit of sharp edges and smooth surfaces that would reflect and refract the light and bewitch the eye.

Across the decades, the jewel was swapped between crowns. It was placed in the crown made for Queen Alexandra, then for Queen Mary, and, more recently, it was in the crown made for the Queen Mother, and it was placed on top of her coffin for her lying-in-state in 2002. Notably, it did not adorn the crowns of any male members of the royal family and this might have partly been due to the superstitious legend that misfortune and calamity would befall any man who coveted the jewel.

The debate about whether the diamond should be returned to India continues today and with some vehemence. Regardless of whether it was intended as a 'gift' at the time, surely the idea of retaining it, and in a crown, is an anachronistic and imperialist position? Yet there are others who argue that there are actually very practical reasons for the diamond remaining where it is. One being that the site of its origin is unknown. If returned, would it be right if it went to India? There are those in Pakistan who have laid claim to it as well, and since its centuries-old provenance can never be known for certain, the right to the diamond remains contentious.

Added to this, it can at least be said that the current custodians are looking after the Koh-i-Noor with an intense amount of security. According to one account, during the Second World War, the authorities and the royal family went above and beyond to secure the treasure. In the event that the Nazis should ever succeed in invading, they made sure they would never find the diamond by taking it to Windsor, sealing it in a box, and lowering that box into a private lake.

These days, the logistics involved in planning, let alone staging, a heist involving the Koh-i-Noor diamond or any of the other Crown Jewels, would surely be prohibitively complex as well as expensive for even the most ambitious thief. In fiction, the idea of a grand robbery at the Tower of London has always required a mastermind. In the 1939 film *The Adventures of Sherlock Holmes*, Basil Rathbone's sleuth found himself in the Tower thwarting a plot by his arch foe, the criminal genius Moriarty. In the updated modern-day TV version, *Sherlock*, Moriarty succeeds in a slightly more devious plot by using the Crown Jewels as bait to lead Holmes into a trap by doing some security camera trickery to show the crown upon his head.

In real life, the only successful attempt to make off with the royal regalia occurred in 1671, and it is a story that is layered with intrigue, both criminological and psychological. Indeed, it has acquired the status of a near legend, despite being wholly true.

The diabolical mastermind at its centre was a career sociopath called Thomas Blood. He was a man, according to those who knew him, of 'down look, lean faced and full of pock-holes'. Born around 1618 in County Clare, Ireland, Blood set sail for England in 1642 in order to throw himself into the English Civil War. According to some, he started out fighting for the king's forces, but it was not long before he swapped sides and instead became a lieutenant in Cromwell's army. He was also a profiteer and a spy on the quiet.

Nonetheless, Blood, who later bestowed upon himself the unearned title 'Colonel', was awarded tranches of land back in Ireland, as well as being made a magistrate. Perhaps this might have satisfied Blood, but then, with the death of Cromwell and the restoration of the monarchy, all his gains were sharply reversed. The lands and the privileges he had acquired were snatched back from him, and now Blood and his wife faced the prospect of stark poverty.

There followed a madcap plot, devised by Blood, to group together with other thwarted Cromwellians, seize Dublin Castle and kidnap the Governor of Ireland, Lord Ormonde. The plan failed and Blood's associates were captured and put to death in short order. And now the 'Colonel' and his wife were fugitives, hiding out in the mountains.

This did not stop them for long. They acquired a new name – Ayloffe – and travelled to England, heedless of the danger of being recognised. They made their way to a small riverside town to the east of London called Romford, where Blood set himself up as an apothecary, dispensing herbal medicines.

Quite where the inspiration to steal the Crown Jewels from the Tower came from is still impossible to say. What *is* known is that, in 1671, the Crown Jewels were guarded by a specially appointed Keeper, Talbot Edwards, who lived at the Tower with his family. Even then the jewels could be viewed by the public, and were kept behind a grille under the watchful eye of Edwards. One day, a parson came to see the treasure. The parson and Edwards struck up friendly conversation, and a rapport which led to further meetings, with the parson bringing his wife to meet Edwards's family. Edwards had a daughter and the parson was desirous she should meet his wealthy nephew. Perhaps romance would blossom? All in all, the Keeper of the Jewels came to value his friendship with the parson greatly. That parson was, of course, Thomas Blood in disguise.

The cruelty of his long-winded plan became clear one morning at the Tower, when the parson came calling with his 'nephew' and two other men. As the 'nephew' paid his compliments to the Keeper's daughter, the 'parson' and his two friends asked to see the Crown Jewels. Edwards, wholly trusting, opened the grille – at which point they set upon him with some violence, stabbing and bludgeoning. They gagged him, tied him up and grabbed their haul, not caring whether the poor keeper lived or died.

Were it not for the violence, Colonel Blood might have been a terrific anti-hero. As it was, the next part of the raid ended in bathos. Some of the royal regalia was stuffed unceremoniously down breeches. Other items were bent or distorted in order to make them easier to carry and hide. Carrying the orb and sceptre and a partly flattened crown, Blood and his accomplices fled across the moat bridge and through the outer gate, but, unfortunately for them, the alarm had already been raised by a visiting Swedish engineer called Martin Beckman. The grievously wounded Edwards had managed to scream, and cry 'Murder! Treason!' when his gag had loosened slightly, so he was swiftly found. And so began a chase through the riverside streets of the city – the ground heavy with dung, the air thick with the smell of fish. Blood did not get far before Tower guards managed to wrestle him to the ground.

What happened next was the first in a series of curious developments. This was a long time before there was any sort of organised police force, but the Tower had its own guards and there were parish magistrates (Colonel Blood had been one himself). But Blood steadfastly refused to submit to any local authorities. He declared that he would give a full account of himself – but only to His Majesty the King.

The effrontery was breath-taking and yet somehow this extraordinary demand was relayed to Charles II. In any earlier era, say under Henry VIII, Blood would surely have simply been taken to the Tower and then executed hideously, but, bizarrely, the king agreed, and said he wanted to see Blood face-to-face. It is not known what passed between them, as Blood stood before the king in chains, but what is certain is that Thomas Blood was pardoned. There have been numerous theories about why this might have been so. Was Charles II simply entertained by the audacity of the crime? Did he admire Colonel Blood's courage and cussedness in requesting this unparalleled audience? Or was it the fact that Charles thought that such a man may prove useful in his employ as a spy? This last theory seemed persuasive to many. Blood, after all, had spent his life hopping from country to country, forming alliances with military figures and then abruptly changing side.

Whatever the case, he now had a pension, and life would otherwise have proceeded tranquilly, had he not been grossly uncivil to the Duke of Buckingham and ended up being sued for everything that he had. Blood, therefore, went to his grave the penniless cussed rogue that he had been throughout much of his life.

Since the Colonel Blood escapade, the Crown Jewels have, by and large, remained secure within their ancient fortress. There have been blips: in 2012, for instance, an opportunist spotted some keys left in an unattended box at the entrance to the Tower and nabbed them. He then used them to get into the precincts at night. But, in an era of CCTV, smartphones and radios, there was little more this figure could do than have a speculative nocturnal adventure within the Tower walls, before scooting out again as the alarm was raised.

So the puzzles in this section will pay tribute to the feats of logistical prowess that the world's most beautiful jewels inspire: the painstakingly intricate ideas hatched by ne'er-do-wells for robberies; and the equally complex skill required to cut stones in such a way that anyone who gazes upon them is left breathless by their beauty. Quite apart from the problem of crowds, there is also a philosophical reason why the guards at the Tower of London keep people moving through the Crown Jewels collection: stop to stare at the Cullinan I diamond too long and you could find yourself hypnotised for the rest of the day.

1

DIAMOND DISCOVERY

Solve the clues on the opposite page and slot the answers in the diamond-shaped grid below. Then, take the letters that appear in the shaded squares and rearrange them to spell out the name of a famous diamond.

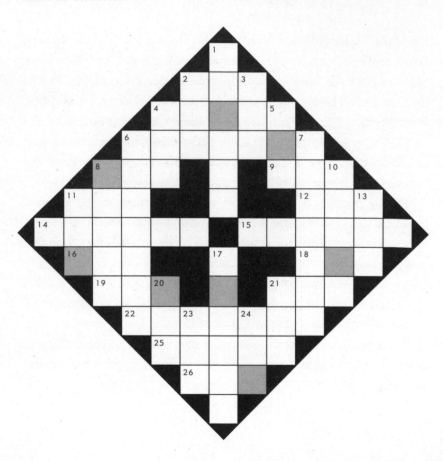

ACROSS

2 Pastry covered dessert (3)

4 Dig deeply (5)

6 Courageously (7)

8 Weep (3)

9 Nourished (3)

11 As well (3)

12 Point at a target (3)

14 Opposite of standing (6)

15 Failed to remember (6)

16 Burned remains (3)

18 Pinch sharply (3)

19 X in Roman numerals (3)

21 Wager (3)

22 Dwelt (7)

25 Signalled with the hand (5)

26 Writing tool (3)

DOWN

1 Precious metal (6)

2 Green vegetable (3)

3 The night before (3)

4 Arid (3)

5 Sprite (3)

6 Male relative (7)

7 Longed for (7)

8 Shoreline (5)

10 Any numeral from 0 to 9 (5)

11 Light afternoon meal (3)

13 Floor cleaner (3)

17 Case for arrows (6)

20 Fresh (3)

21 Garden plot (3)

23 Plant juice (3)

24 Lion's lair (3)

2

A PAIR OF RINGS

Fit the listed words back into their correct places in the two ring grids. The last two letters of one word are the first two of the next, and all words have five letters and are written in a clockwise direction. However there are only eighteen words here and you need ten to complete each ring, making twenty words in all. A word connected with jewels and jewellery is missing from each ring. Can you work out what it is?

To start you off, two letters are already set in place in the rings. In RING 1 the third letter of answer word 1 is G. In RING 2 the third letter of answer word 1 is V.

ALONE
ANGEL
AZURE
CACTI
CELLO
CHIME
DEUCE
ELOPE
ERODE
GEESE
LOTTO
MECCA
NEVER
PEACH
RANGE
REBUS
SEDAN
USUAL

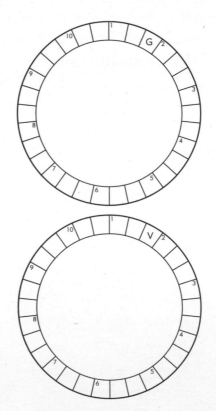

3

SYMBOLS

Symbols have taken the place of letters in these gemstones. The substitution is consistent throughout all of the names. Can you name the gems?

1   ✶   ☆   ✡   ★

2   ☆   ✚   ✡   ✳   ★

3   ✚   ★   ✚   ✳   ✡   ☆   ♣

4   ✳   ✡   ☆   ☆   ★   ☆   ✳   ✚

5   ♣   ☆   ✡   ★   ★   ✳   ♣

4

CORONATION QUIZ

A Royal Coronation is when the splendid Crown Jewels leave the Tower for a short while.

Test your knowledge of Coronations in the twentieth century. Don't look at the answers until you have attempted all the questions.

1   Which two Coronation years of the twentieth century have the same total when each digit in the year is added up?

2   Of the twentieth century Coronation years, which gives the highest number when the digits of the year are added together?

3   Who is the only monarch of the twentieth century to have been crowned in a year which contains an even number?

5

THE JEWEL HOUSE

Five visitors to the Tower have chosen to visit the world-famous Jewel House, the home of the Crown Jewels. Anne, Elizabeth, Kate, Philip and William each step on to the moving walkway one at a time. Using the information below can you say in which order they did this, which item of the Coronation Regalia each preferred and what their favourite precious gem was?

1   Diamonds, emeralds, pearls, rubies and sapphires were the five favourite gems. Only one visitor prefers a gem whose initial letter is the same as the first letter of their name.

2   Ampulla, Imperial State Crown, Orb, Sceptre and St Edward's Crown were the five favourite items of Coronation Regalia.

3   The person who liked the St Edward's Crown and had pearls as favourite gem was the fifth and last of the group to visit the jewel house.

4   Kate, who wasn't first, went before the person who liked diamonds, who in turn went before the person who liked sapphires.

5   Philip was particularly impressed by the sceptre. He followed directly behind Anne.

6   The person who liked the Ampulla went directly before the person who liked the State Crown.

7   Orb and rubies were not paired together as favourite by anyone in the group.

6

CROWN MAKING

The children from a local primary school have visited the Tower as part of their history curriculum. So impressed were they with the Crown Jewels that on their return to school a group of them decide to make their own versions of a Royal crown. A third of the 'jewels' they used were 'rubies', a fifth were 'emeralds' and forty-nine were 'sapphires.' How many 'jewels' were used in the design?

CHAPTER NINE

STAR CHARTS AND MYSTERIOUS SYMBOLS

THERE is a dark and tight spiral staircase built into a round turret of the White Tower. It rises from the basement, with doorways for each of the tower's floors, and ascends finally into the roof of the turret. In 1675, this was still one of the loftiest look-out points in the city. But for one inspirational young man – his knees and elbows creaking painfully with rheumatic fever – these stairs were also a gruelling trial. He had to haul heavy brass astronomical equipment up to the summit. For this was the very first Royal Observatory and the young man, John Flamsteed, was the very first Astronomer Royal.

He was a brilliant mathematician fired with the poetry of the distant heavens, but he had a very practical job to do too. This was a time when international trade was booming, however the ships sailing those mighty oceans, under vast night skies, still had no completely reliable system of navigation. Part of Flamsteed's commission was to help solve this riddle.

And, in this sense, his purpose fitted the ethos of the Tower of London very neatly. For elsewhere in that White Tower, in the exquisite chapel facing the river, was an ever-growing and invaluable repository of knowledge, in the shape of ancient legal scrolls and parchments: the historic heart of the nation was kept here. This was the nerve centre of a new and modern civic life and, again, this was because the nation was becoming ever more of a global powerhouse. The Tower stood firmly as the anchor for this new empire. These invaluable documents, stored all around the eleventh-century chapel, were every bit as esoteric as the maps of the heavens that Flamsteed was charting: they recorded the minutiae of national life while he recorded the tiny twinkling stars.

So, the puzzles in this section will have that blend of celestial wonder and logistical doggedness; the complexities and symbols of ancient records next to high-flown cosmic patterns. A mixture of soaring imagination combined with an earthly practicality.

The very idea of appointing a full-time astronomer to devote his nights to staring into the unfathomable velvet darkness was prompted by Charles II's mistress of the time, and by the fear that European competitors might be getting ahead of the game. In France, astronomers were working to find the key to calculating longitude by the stars. Ships at that time were still veering disastrously off course on long ocean voyages, and quite apart from questions of crew safety, there was the burning profit motive. With proper navigation, ships could slash sailing times, and the flow of goods from nation to nation would be ever faster.

This was a new age of rationality and calculation. In London, the Royal Society had been established, bringing together men of learning with interests in all kinds of disciplines. Born and educated in Derbyshire, John Flamsteed had come to the attention of the Society for his mathematical skill. He also had a knack for fine instrumentation and had made a barometer from brass that had been presented to Charles II.

And so it was that Flamsteed was awarded a salary of £100 a year – something close to the sum of £14,000 now (though such sums went much further then) – and with which he was expected to buy and create his own equipment, in order to join the race to unravel longitude. The Tower of London was never intended as a permanent home; rather, it was his base while the purpose-built Royal Observatory in Greenwich, five miles downriver, was being constructed.

Nonetheless, the young man might have found his domain within this ancient and historic castle rather pleasing. The first of his heavenly observations from the round tower was made in April 1675. And it might have been for the best that he worked in the White Tower in relative solitude anyway, for Flamsteed had a molten temper and was a great hater of rivals. He especially loathed fellow astronomer Edmund Halley, whose name was to become immortalised by the comet he discovered, and who succeeded Flamsteed as Astronomer Royal.

And Flamsteed's footsteps through the Tower precincts thankfully pre-dated those of Sir Isaac Newton, whom he also cordially detested. Newton wanted very specific observations from Flamsteed, concerning the orbit of the moon, which was to do with his work on gravity. For Flamsteed, these requests were inexplicable and hugely irritating. His gaze was fixed immovably on the celestial mathematical beauty of the planets and stars beyond.

According to some accounts, however, there was an even more pervasive infuriation at the top of the White Tower, because Flamsteed's telescopes were constantly harassed by the Tower's ravens. Flamsteed specifically petitioned the king for permission to have the beautiful black birds killed, but, given the legend of what would befall the Tower and the kingdom were the ravens to ever leave, this intemperate demand was denied. Another story has it that the astronomer spent a great deal of time shooing away other varieties of curious birds.

Flamsteed's feuds continued with some energy after he had moved from the Tower to the hill at Greenwich, but they were nothing compared to another of the Tower's most famous figures, who had walked these precincts a few years previously. The rigid and ferocious puritan William Prynne, appointed Keeper of Records in 1660, suffered grievously for his outspoken beliefs throughout his life, but, in turn, he also visited great suffering upon others.

Prynne had actually been a prisoner in the Tower for some years and was an emblem of the bloody confusion of the English Civil War. His early career had been a ceaseless confrontation with authority, so it was ironic that, in his latter years, he was the man who actually brought the greatest semblance of order to all the royal, civic and legal documents with which the Tower of London was stuffed. Born in the west country in 1600, he was exceptionally bright and compulsively argumentative. After university, he became a lawyer. But he had also found religion, and a very particular branch of religion at that. England during the reign of James I, and then Charles I, was settling into its own form of Protestantism, but the rising Puritan sect – which abominated everything from alcohol to theatre to long hair on men – took against this established church, seeing it as filled with fripperies and suspecting that its clerics were too close to Popery.

And so William Prynne, both fixated and narrow-eyed, began writing fiery and relentless pamphlets against what he saw as the evils of the age. In 1633, he wrote a 900-page rant concerning the immoral squalor of theatre, and of the women who acted upon the stage. This was at a point when Charles I's wife, Queen Henrietta Maria, had herself taken to the stage in a royal masque. Prynne's widely published howl of rage drew him to the attention of the Star Chamber, the body of men who judged upon matters of treason. He was found guilty, and not only fined a huge sum of money and sentenced to imprisonment in the Tower, he also had to suffer a horrible physical punishment. Prynne was placed inside wooden stocks and held there as his ears were 'clipped' with sharp blades. 'Clipping' meant that they were partly hacked off. His time as a Tower prisoner began.

However, if the authorities imagined that a bare cell in the Wakefield Tower would temper his need to denounce his betters, they were quite wrong. Prynne continued writing, his Puritan faith implacably opposed to what he saw as the vanities of the age, as represented by Archbishop Laud, whom he loathed. The provocations became too sulphurous and Prynne was sentenced to suffer even more drastic punishment. The remainder of his ears were sawn off, his nostrils were slit and red hot irons in the shapes of the letters 'S' and 'L' were pressed into the flesh of his cheeks. The letters stood for 'Seditious Liar' and the intention was that the scars would be there for the rest of his life.

But the turmoil of the times meant that all manner of men were swept up on unexpected tides. Long a Tower prisoner, Prynne was released in 1640 as the thunderclouds of civil war gathered, and he even became an MP. He set off in fiery pursuit of evidence against Archbishop Laud, and Laud was eventually executed.

Yet soon Prynne's granite and unyielding faith, which saw human sin in every public figure, caused him to turn against Oliver Cromwell and those who had beheaded the king, so he was back in that Tower prison again. In 1660, though, the wheel had turned finally on the republicans and the monarchy was restored. And, curiously, Prynne, who by then had been deemed supportive to Charles II, was rewarded with the lucrative position of Keeper of Records at the Tower. What had once been his prison was now, for him, a storehouse of delight.

The Records were one of the nerve centres of the realm. Without all these scrolls, parchments, contracts and other diverse documents, the entire nation would have been cast into a sort of lawless confusion. The most urgent problem – apart from a genuinely efficient means of filing – was space. Since around the 1200s, the Wakefield Tower had been home to all this invaluable and irreplaceable paperwork. But it was full. And so a new home was found in the unlikely setting of the Chapel of St John, at the top of the White Tower. The chapel, with its beautiful Romanesque arches, had galleries which overlooked the altar and the nave. These were deemed suitable for the piling up of scrolls. Other documents were quite literally flattened with a pressing contraption before being filed.

But among all these faded scrolls was the shadow history of the nation. What an extraordinary library for anyone to be able to plough through. And Prynne, whose days were once filled with righteous fury, seemed to find some peace as he moved around the Tower precincts. It was observed that he wore a quilted cap, which partly covered or shielded his eyes.

And what complexities he faced when handling medieval documentation from centuries back, for that era was wildly abundant in symbolism. The nature of an old record might be deciphered not from a category card but from a small hieroglyph. One example was that of a small picture of grape-pressing. This would denote that here was a document to do with revenues gathered from the wine region of Bordeaux. Added to this was the endlessly varied imagery used on wax seals: the grander royal variety were large, and might depict the king of the time riding into battle, or seated on a throne, giving a lawmaker's judgments. Then there was the medieval passion for illumination and decoration, and so there were rich golds, reds and blues swirling around carefully inscribed parchments, and, of course, this was more symbolism. The authority of the document was often conveyed by the thickness of the parchment, which was made from animal hides.

Some two hundred years after Prynne's custodianship, there came the point in the early Victorian era when the Tower authorities realised that there was simply no more room for this extraordinary repository of national history. On top of this, there was the ever-present fear of fire. In the old days, valuable charters and royal documents had been kept near, or in, chapels, because these were regarded as ultimate bastions of safety. But in the event of a major conflagration, of which there were several within the Tower precincts, most notably in 1841, then centuries of history might be reduced to ashes.

In 1838, the decision was made to store the documents more securely and, ten years later, all preparations and construction complete, this vast archive was transported with the greatest care to a new purpose-built archive in the city, which became known as the Public Record Office. It too became too small for this treasure in time. And, these days, the rolls of parchment with the wax seals that had been tended by the Tower's medieval archivists are now lodged safely within the temperature-controlled environment of The National Archives at Kew. Parchments from almost one thousand years ago, especially those that have been kept properly throughout the centuries, look as fresh and dazzling and authoritative as they did when they were first drawn up. The Tower, for centuries, had been home to the memory of the nation.

And so the puzzles in this section will reflect both the wonderfully inventive symbolism of the medieval mind, and will also lift our eyes to the heavens, as they take some inspiration from the Tower's irascible first Astronomer Royal, and his quest to understand cosmic gravity while fighting off pigeons.

1

STAR CROSSED

In the seventeenth century, the White Tower was still one of London's tallest buildings. This meant it was an ideal base for observing the night sky and therefore attracted leading scientists of the time.

Below is a list of words with a scientific link, in no particular order. The letters in the words have been rearranged in alphabetical order. Unravel the words, slot them into their correct places in the 7 × 7 square, and the diagonal reading top left to bottom right will reveal the name of the monarch who appointed the first Astronomer Royal, whose telescope was placed at the White Tower.

CHIPSSY   EEHMORT

ACMOPSS   CEHIMST

AAELNSY   AELMPSS

AEINRTT

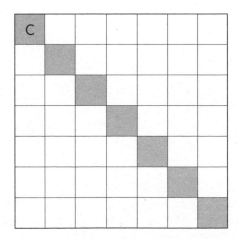

2

IN ORBIT

Planet X takes two years to orbit the Sun.

Planet Y takes four years to orbit the Sun.

Planet Z takes eight years to orbit the Sun.

When will all three planets next be in line with the Sun?

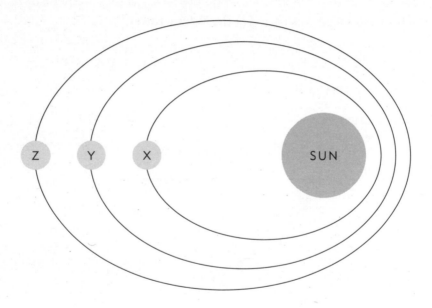

3

PARCHMENT PUZZLE

The Tower was once the home of official record keeping. The earliest items would be drawn on pieces of parchment. If a copy was needed then the work would have to be drawn out again by hand. Several copies have been made of parchments that contain a series of strange-looking symbols. Three copies are identical. Which three?

4

SYMBOLIC

These strange-looking symbols may look like they are of ancient significance. In fact they could be used when filing away papers this very day.

Which of the shapes, 1, 2, 3 or 4, continues the pattern?

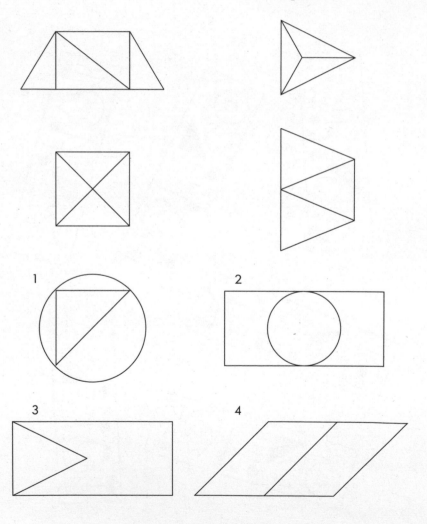

5

THE YEAR IN QUESTION

The grid below contains shapes linked to studying the stars and astronomy. Each symbol represents a digit from 1 to 7. You are given the total value in each horizontal row and each vertical column. What digit does each symbol represent?

When you have solved this, see if you can work out what year is represented by a white star, a ringed planet, a black star and a cloud of cosmic dust. Why was this year important in the world of astronomy and its links with the Tower of London?

19	☁	☆	○	☁	○
15	●	◉	☆	◉	★
18	◉	🪐	☆	★	◉
16	●	★	◉	☆	●
20	☆	★	☆	○	★
■	14	23	9	19	23

A TOUCH OF LUXURY

RISING from the medieval kitchens situated beneath the Wakefield Tower were appetite-sharpening aromas coming from the rich and varied ingredients used therein. And these aromas would have been detected in the sumptuous chambers within which Henry III – and, later, Edwards I to III – reposed. There was a time when the Tower of London was intended to provide homely and pleasing quarters not only for royalty, but also senior members of the royal household. The attention to detail in the rugs, the curtains, the bed linens, the brightly painted walls, the rich clothing, and also in the golden cutlery used at feasts, was intense and acute. There was nothing dour about medieval royalty, and it seemed there was no end to the medieval taste for dazzle and novelty.

So the puzzles in this section will be infused with that aesthetic flair. Here are conundrums involving weaves and threads and elaborate designs and heralds, and brainteasers involving the harum-scarum logistics of royal banquets, and the best and fastest routes by which the most deliciously elaborate dishes could be conveyed to the royal parties upstairs.

The original Norman invaders never quite reached the pitch of enjoyable (and cosy) indulgence that their successors enjoyed. William the Conqueror's heirs in the 1100s occupied the White Tower, which, while architecturally impressive, was also a forbidding prospect of high ceilings and vast chambers. Their living space was in the upper floors, close to the Chapel of St John. It is thought their servants lived and worked on the first floor. There was no integral kitchen, so food was prepared just outside the fortress in a small out-building, and brought in.

By the reign of Henry III in the late 1200s, royal entertaining was more lavish, and the ingredients surprisingly varied. At times, the quantities of meat that were cooked and consumed was scarcely imaginable. In one account, a Christmas feast held by Henry featured 1,300 hares, 200 wild swine, 830 deer and, strikingly, 115 cranes. These were accompanied by over one thousand gallons of wine. The old movie image of a fat medieval monarch gnawing at a vast leg-bone wasn't far off the mark. But that said, at the Tower, as at other royal palaces, the preparation of food was every bit as delicate an art as it is now, even in an era long before any kind of refrigeration or, indeed, temperature-controlled ovens.

By the medieval period, the river wharves clustered around the Tower were bobbing with boats filled with spices. Cardamom and cloves were to be found in the Tower kitchens, together with garlic, ginger, cinnamon and nutmeg. There was subtlety in sauces.

But, if the king's plate was piled high with partridges, it was not purely for reasons of greed, rather it was the custom for the monarch to hand his food over to favoured subjects at the table. There were rich stews, made with pork or veal, bacon fat, onions, almonds, white wine, pepper, cloves and saffron. The winter appetite for pies was strong, and one medieval recipe for 'Great Pie' featured venison, pheasant and rabbit, onions, garlic, bacon, chicken stock, a hefty slosh of Merlot and the juice of an orange.

The Tower's kitchens would have been daunting environments; swelteringly hot, filled with blades and meat-hooks, and the sweat of seriously ill-tempered labourers. There were dishes that would seem quite alien to us now: for example, a form of blancmange, mentioned by Chaucer, which involved stiff white custard made with almond milk and garnished with chicken. Another example was a speciality of Richard II's cooks: a sweet-and-sour meat stew. This stew contained chicken and pork, together with the livers of the bird and the pig, all chopped and ground into a paste, blended with broth, thickened with egg yolks and seasoned with a judicious blend of ginger, saffron and sugar.

Indeed, it was Richard's cooks who bequeathed the world one of the very first recipe books, known as *The Forme of Cury* ('cury' then meant cooking). Here were details for cooking whales and porpoises, seals and herons. But amid the more extravagant ingredients, there were also items such as olive oil, and recipes for more everyday fare, such as pork in sage sauce, or toasted bread doused in a mixture of honey and wine, or braised pumpkin in saffron.

Feasts in the medieval tower were also accompanied by extraordinary edible sculptures. There were jelly castles with great towers, and sugar ships and eagles. Sometimes different courses were arranged around particular colour schemes, with dishes made in green and gold, or bold red, not only carrying all sorts of different symbolic weight, but also satisfying that medieval desire for rich colours all around.

In the Tudor period, when the Tower seemed more of a prison than a castle, food was either cooked on the premises or else brought in from the outside. And the recipes had developed a little more. There was baked salmon with onion strips, garnished with violets and served with oil and vinegar, as an example of the way that aristocratic households used flowers (though not their toxic roots) artfully as attractive and edible decoration. Side dishes could be inventive too. Popular in the late 1500s was asparagus in orange sauce (involving the juice of around half a dozen oranges, brown sugar and butter). Also lauded in contemporary recipe tracts was the dish of sweet potatoes in rose and orange sauce (similar to the above, but this was decorated with the addition of rose petals, when in season).

The medieval occupants of the Tower, as well as delighting in the rich colour of their food, gave careful thought to other comforts. Edward I had intricate glazing installed in the Wakefield Tower, giving the riverside bedchamber insulation from the winds and noise of the river. His bed was furnished with the finest linen and coverings and, later, in the reign of Richard II, as Clerk of the King's Works, the poet Geoffrey Chaucer was to see for himself the fine 'feather bed' plumped with 'many a pillow'. The hangings around the bed, and draped upon the walls, were dense in the complex patterns of heraldic quatrefoils. And the intricacy of such patterns could also be found in the Tower's floor tiles and other details, and they were replicated in the clothes that succeeding monarchs wore too. These royal robes and cloaks and tunics, and the myriad other items that festooned the royal person, were kept in a section of the precinct called the Wardrobe Tower.

These items of silk and velvet, wool and fur, were kept not far from the Tower's garderobe, which was another word for a latrine. The theory, in the early Middle Ages, was that the thick miasma arising from the pit would deter moths. The villainous King John was assiduous about adding to his wardrobe and adorning himself in all the finery of majesty. His was an age in which scarlet cloth was a distinct luxury and furs were appropriated from a variety of animals, down to the smallest squirrels. The fur of the stoat was prized for its softness, particularly its winter coat, which could be white with a black tip to the tail, and was used to create ermine trimming that can still be seen today, for example, in archive shots of the assembled House of Lords ('ermine' is another name for stoat).

The Middle Ages was a time of the strictest sumptuary laws. Clothing for all classes was strictly regulated, so that no one would be seen to be climbing above their station. The king's stewards, therefore, wore black, while huntsmen wore green. The items in the king's wardrobe could only ever be worn by the monarch, and these included long red robes lined with emerald silk with coats bedazzled with gold lacework. The King's Wardrobe – a term which expanded to encompass all royal valuables and spending too – was also the repository for what might be termed the king's accessories. In the case of King John, these were not strictly Crown Jewels but also more frivolous items. There were lances painted with gold leaf and a long staff set with almost two dozen deep-blue sapphires. There was also a silver cabinet set with a variety of flashing stones.

But this was not mere vanity or frivolity on King John's part, for clothes and appearance, both of the monarch and of the lords and servants who attended him, were of the highest symbolic importance in medieval England. They denoted both power and unity. For instance, if the king's retinue was on royal progress to another part of the country, it was essential that all of those in the royal party looked both smart and perfectly uniform. In 1301, the Keeper of the Great Wardrobe sent the following message to the master of the stores, who ordered up materials: 'Because there are sixteen valets who [. . .] follow the king every day on the road, which valets are badly dressed, I order you to deliver to them, of the king's gift, four cloths of a suit'. Moreover, through much of the medieval period, there was something resembling a copyright law on styles and colours that only the king and his chosen attendants were allowed to wear. For instance, Henry II banned the general use of scarlet, sable (the fur from a small eastern European marten), vair (the fur from the back of a squirrel) and gris (also squirrel fur, but from many squirrels, and luxuriously stitched together into a sort of patterned fur quilt).

Different kings favoured different colour schemes. At Christmas in 1214, for example, all the knights at the court of King John were robed in a uniform of green cloth. In later years, the colour scheme varied from brilliant white to ash grey, from russet and cinnamon to blue.

Colour was as much an indicator of wealth as jewellery and, in the Middle Ages, some pigment dyes were much more expensive than others. But, gradually, there were innovations in producing new colours, and also new fashions to display several colours all in one garment. This was most strikingly seen in a revolt led by a nobleman, Roger Mortimer, the Earl of March.

As we have learned, during the reign of Edward II, in the early 1300s, Mortimer dramatically fell out of love with his monarch, hating his favouritism towards the Despenser family. Mortimer assembled an army of rebels and this army was noted for its striking and colourful uniform. These were tunics of green and yellow, with white flashes on the arm. The effect of this bright uniformity was intimidation, and it spoke not only of solidarity, but the colours were also a startling contrast with the more sombre shades of the king's defenders. In essence, there was almost a punk element to them, in terms of outrage. In time, Mortimer was forced to surrender and, as we have seen, was sent to the Tower, from which he escaped. But it was interesting that his challenge was rendered symbolically in this shocking fashion statement.

The Royal Wardrobe went through one of its most extravagant phases during the reign of Richard II, who was a great lover of art, architecture and, indeed, fashion. One of the more curious footnotes in his story is the claim that the young king invented the handkerchief. The Royal Wardrobe accounts showed, for the very first time, expenditure on special squares of linen designed to be applied to the nose. Added to this, the king understood about the impact of court dress. His tailor made him 'a tunic of pearls and other precious stones and gold' and he had a specially designed costume to be worn at a grand masque or ball. This consisted of a tunic and doublet embroidered with extraordinary symbols: 'water' and 'rocks' delineated in silk, and 'fifteen whelks and fifteen mussels of silver gilt' and 'fifteen cockles of white silver'. It also had embroidered 'gold orange trees' and 'oranges of silver gilt'.

Richard II even had costumes made for falconry expeditions, and for wearing to ceremonial tournaments. There were velvet mantles, gold pendants, chains of ermine fashioned to look like vines, and all bedecked with what might be described as the king's self-selected logo: the white hart (or deer). This he sometimes wore as a brooch set with rubies, but the symbol was also worn by senior members of his court, although in their case sewn on to sleeves and tunics, as opposed to glittering with jewels. Here was a king who understood very well the potency of the Great Wardrobe and what such opulent clothes signified, not just to the general population, but also to foreign kings and dignitaries. Here was a display of status that carried across oceans. However, it was also, in part, what fuelled distrust in Richard's reign. It was often seen as overt favouritism when some of the court were allowed to wear certain garments, and this alienated other lords, a symbolic insult that helped contribute to his miserable downfall.

With the advent of Henry IV, the term 'wardrobe' had regenerated again. This was now a department that, as well as storing treasures, also had the power to issue and raise finances for the king. Then, with the Tudors, came the first inklings of what would evolve into the Civil Service. The Wardrobe itself outgrew the Tower and was moved to new premises in the City: the site (though not the building) can be found at Wardrobe Place.

And as royal activity moved away from the Tower, what was left was the residual memory of the brightest finery kept in vast cold stone chambers and of jewels flashing and gleaming in the darkness. Today, the modern Tower honours the aesthetic history of the Tower's royal heritage. As the recreations of Edward I's bedchamber and throne room and chapel show, the Tower opens a window into the royal comforts of the past, and into the furnishings and decorations and even the table settings that pleased kings and queens the most. So, the puzzles in this section have that swirl of indulgence and require a keen eye for heraldic symbols and the rich complexities of medieval cooking.

1

QUIZ QUOTE

Answer the quiz questions below linked to the Tower and write the answers across in the upper grid on the opposite page. When this is completed, take the letters in the keycoded squares and slot them into their correct places in the smaller grid. Column A, reading down, will reveal the name of a character in a musical work set in the Tower, and the keycoded letters will reveal a quote by him from the operetta.

1 Who guarded the prisoners when the Tower was used as a prison?
2 Which form of combat used bows and arrows?
3 One is of St John the Evangelist, another is of St Peter ad Vincula and has Royal added to its name; what are they?
4 What is the area ruled by a monarch called?
5 Which big cat was one of many who lived at the Tower and is illustrated in an eighteenth-century book for children?
6 What name was given to fugitives from justice?
7 In 1800 a gun salute took place at the Tower to celebrate the union between Great Britain and which country?
8 Which invaders accompanied William the Conqueror when he triumphed over King Harold?
9 Which brass instrument can be used for a fanfare?

	A	B	C	D	E	F	G
1							
2							
3							
4							
5							
6							
7							
8							
9							

G9	D2	E3	B7	E1		B4	G8		B3	B6	G4	B8	C9	F2		C1	C5	

E8	D6	D7	

A9	E5	A7	F8	D4	G1	

2

WORD TOWER

The Tower is famously a fortress, a palace and a prison. In this puzzle we give you one of those words to start you off: PALACE. Find the answers to the clues and slot them in the tower grid. They are in no particular order. Each answer is an anagram of the word above or below it, with one letter added or one taken away. The letters in the shaded squares will give you the name of another Tower building – in fact there are two.

Playing card with a single symbol

Location, site

Division of a book

Speed contest

Appease, calm down

Royal residence

Deliver a sermon

Stretch out the hand

Delicate, ornamental trimming or fabric

3

HERALDIC COLOURS

Colours used in heraldry complete the first clue below and start the second clue.

1 Rhode Island (_____) Admiral

2 Prussian (_____) Bottle

3 Fools' (_____) Digger

4 Penny (_____) Market

5 Tower (_____) House

6 Quick (_____) Screen

7 Dog (_____) Hip

8 Royal (_____) Patch

4

FAMILY CREST

A new family crest is to take pride of place in the Banqueting Hall. From the information below can you say which shield is the correct one?

There are more black squares than white ones.

There is an odd number of swords, and their points face inwards.

In the quarter with black vertical stripes a black stripe is nearest to the outer edge.

The raven is looking to his right.

No quarter contains a triangle.

5

CHEERS

Fine wine would flow freely at the splendid banquets on special occasions at the Tower. Three noble lords have boasted of their expertise in being able to name any wine that is given to them. A challenge is arranged and seven different wines, which we will refer to as A, B, C, D, E, F and G, are served in goblets to the wine experts. They know the names of the wines, but they don't know the order in which they will be served. Lord Elpless is convinced that the order was B, A, C, G, E, D, F. Lord Blanc de Blanc believes the order was D, C, B, A, G, F, E. Lord Rouge doesn't remember too much after the final tasting but his recollection is that the order was B, C, E, F, D, A, G. Every wine has been correctly identified by at least one of the Lords. Each Lord correctly named three of the wines.

In which order were the wines served?

6

FOOD SHARE

A table at a medieval banquet has been set out below. There are six different items connected with luxurious food and drink. There's a bottle of wine, a goblet, a platter, a pie, a goose and a pear. Your job is to divide the contents of the table into six equal portions, with each portion containing six different items.

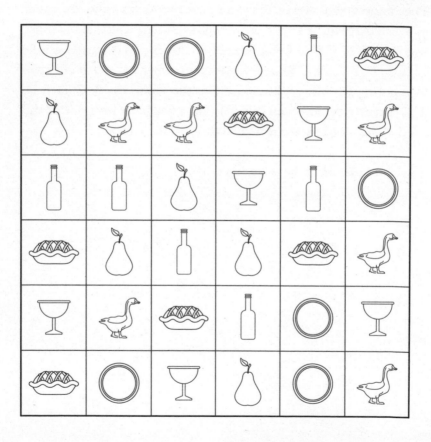

7

MEDIEVAL BANQUET

Sumptuous banquets were a means of impressing one's neighbours as well as providing nourishment. A mixture of different birds or animals, reared or caught on the lord's estate, might be included in a pie flavoured with exotic spices. The names of some such ingredients are listed below, but the letters in the names have been mixed up and rearranged in alphabetical order. Can you sort them out?

1   A N S W

2   A A E H N P S T

3   A B D I L O R W (two words)

4   A D E G I P R R T

5   E I N N O S V

6   C E L O S V

7   E G G I N R

8   A A C D M M O R

9   A F F N O R S

10   E G M N T U

CHAPTER ELEVEN

CEREMONIES AND RAVENS

AS A uniform, it is at once ornate, colourful, unique and faintly preposterous. Perhaps this is why it is such a perfect symbol for Britain itself. It is a costume rooted deep in a fantasy past, which nonetheless projects a reassuring sense of continuity and bluff friendliness. The Yeoman Warders of the Tower of London, more familiarly known as 'Beefeaters', because of a legend about the dishes they were permitted, have patrolled the Tower's precincts for over five hundred years. Theirs is a world of fascinating and arcane ceremonies and rituals involving keys and responses. The world that they inhabit is one that seems, in some ways, removed from the everyday tides of time.

And as these men (and now women) preside over this delightfully esoteric world, they also take care of some of the Tower's other more eccentric features, most notable among which are the ravens, which stay within the Tower's grounds and amusingly glare at the countless tourists who seek to take selfies with them every day.

So, the puzzles in this section will involve a certain amount of complicated tradition: keys, locks and the routes of midnight patrols. There will also be some headscratchers that pay tribute to the keen intelligence of the ravens, well known to be formidable problem-solving birds. Can you match your wits against those of your corvid friends when it comes to logic conundrums about obtaining nuts from seemingly enclosed spaces?

The reason that the Yeoman (or Beefeater) uniform is so intensely particular and unique is that it was a creation of the Tudor period. It is thought that Henry VII introduced the principle of soldiers specially assigned to duties at the Tower in the late 1400s, but it was under his son, Henry VIII, that they acquired their distinct character. In his reign, they were intended as personal bodyguards and soldiers, who would be on permanent alert for any kind of attack on the Tower or on the king.

And this is where the astonishing costume of red and gold, with scarlet tights and shoes and bonnets festooned with flowers and ribbons, found its genesis. On normal days, the Yeoman Warders wear what is called the 'undress' uniform of dark blue piped with bright red stripes. But on state occasions, the full Tudor ensemble is on display.

They wear doublets of embroidered scarlet cloth and tights of scarlet merino, over which are worn breeches of scarlet cloth, with gold garters at the knee – plus red, white and blue ribbons at the knee too. These ribbons also appear in the black velvet Tudor bonnets, and also on the patent-leather Oxford shoes. There are magnificent ruffs, fashioned from frills of white linen, white cotton gloves, a sword belt and, for the more sombre state occasions, cloaks of dark blue lined with scarlet silk. The over-all effect is anachronistic but also unquestionably dignified. In the precincts of the Tower now, when the Beefeaters are in their simpler dark blue pleated doublets, there is absolutely no questioning their authority. If any tourist unwisely tries to sneak underneath a rope barrier – or even enters the Chapel of St Peter ad Vincula without removing their hat – the Yeoman Warders let them know very sharply that they are transgressing.

They always were rather firm, despite the Ruritanian jolliness of the uniform. The American novelist Nathaniel Hawthorne, visiting London in the 1850s, was very interested to see the Crown Jewels. But, as he recalled, the time he could spend examining their fine detail was limited, as the Yeoman Warders were insistently moving him along.

They used to be even flintier than that. In 1536, some two hundred of these richly attired men were outside St Peter ad Vincula, on sentry guard duty, when Anne Boleyn was executed. Five hundred years later, in the present day, it is curious to look at those who wear these distinctive clothes and imagine them in an altogether graver light.

The Yeoman Warders are exceptionally aware of their own history, of course, and proudly maintain the centuries-old traditions that go with it. The most famous and the oldest is the Ceremony of the Keys, and it has a curious origin. It was in the 1300s that the then king, Edward III, arrived at the Tower one winter night, unannounced, his plans having changed. But the monarch was, in turn, surprised. Instead of finding guards at the moat gate, the entire fortress appeared to be entirely unmanned. He rode straight through, into the heart of the Tower precincts, without once being challenged.

The implications for the night-time security of the royal apartments in the Wakefield Tower were not good and Edward was so angry that he had the Constable of the Tower arrested and imprisoned. This led to an entire review of the defences of the Tower as well as procuring of funds from the sheriffs of London to improve the fortifications, and it was at this point that the king introduced the Ceremony of the Keys. As the sun set on each day, the entire Tower of London was to be locked up; and then re-opened at sunrise.

But it was Queen Mary, some two centuries later, who made sure that the ceremony was conducted with more rigid formality, and by this time, it was to be carried out by the Yeoman Warders in their bright uniforms. The rules were laid out in a document, which read: 'And it is ordered that there shall be a place appointed under Locke and key where in the keys of the gates of the saide tower shall be laid in the sight of the constable, the porter, and two of the yeoman warders, or three of them at the least, and by two or three of them to be taken out when they shall be occupied. And the key of that locke or coffer where the keys be, to be kepte by the porter, or in his absence, by the chief yeoman warder.'

The timing of the ceremony remained unchanged until the early nineteenth century, when the first Duke of Wellington, in his capacity as Tower constable, was stationed there with some of his men. He decreed that the hour of lockdown should be moved to 10 p.m., to ensure that all his troops were back within the Tower walls. The ceremony that is carried out now is essentially the same as the one dating back hundreds of years, albeit with that minor change to timing. And now, with prior appointment, it is possible to watch it unfold.

At seven minutes to ten o'clock each night, the Chief Yeoman Warder emerges from the Bayward Tower. He is in his full scarlet array, together with the velvet Tudor bonnet. In one hand is an old-fashioned lantern, with glass sides, containing a single burning candle to illuminate his path. In the other hand is the set of what are called 'the Queen's keys' (when Prince Charles inherits the throne, they will once more become 'the King's'). The Chief Yeoman Warder processes down through the darkness to the Bloody Tower, where he is met by a contingent of sentries. Among them is a drummer and a bugler. Together, they make their way to the Tower's outer gate, across what was the moat. There the Yeoman carries out the locking-up while the others stand guard.

All of this is timed so precisely that, at the stroke of 10 p.m., as the lock is turned, the Yeoman then declares: 'God preserve Queen Elizabeth'. And the bugler strikes up the 'Last Post'. The ceremonial group then take the keys to the Queen's House to be given to the Resident Governor.

Another Tower of London tradition – this one rather noisier and certainly more public – is that of the gun salute. Mounted guns (naturally not firing projectiles!) point out from Tower Wharf to the river. On occasions of royal celebration, the guns fire sixty-two rounds: the reason is that twenty-one rounds are specifically for the royal element, an additional twenty are in honour of the Tower's position as a royal palace and an additional twenty-one rounds are fired to acknowledge the City of London. The most recent examples of this ceremonial firepower came with the births of the children of the Duke and Duchess of Cambridge – Prince George, Princess Charlotte and Prince Louis – and the echoing, resonating roar of the guns is always impressive for visitors. The occasion of the Queen's birthday is also marked in the same way, with the deep thunder stretching out across ten minutes.

And this is a tradition that also stretches back a startlingly long way. It started in the Tudor era. The first recorded instance of guns being fired in celebration at the Tower happened upon the coronation of Anne Boleyn as queen. Did she recall the deep booms of that day when, not very long afterwards, she faced her darkest hours in the Tower?

Some other ceremonies are a little more eccentric. An old custom involving the cheerful consumption of wine continues to this day: the Constable's Dues. On the occasion of a Royal Navy vessel sailing up the Thames, past Tower Bridge and the Tower, it must pay a form of tribute and this always comes in the shape of a barrel of wine. The captain of the ship comes ashore at the Tower Wharf, and the barrel is presented to the Yeoman Warders. Naval personnel then carry the wine up to the Resident Governor's office at the Queen's House. And there the barrel is cracked open.

Yet this particular tradition is an evolved version of what used to be rather a valuable bonus for the Constable of the Tower in the Middle Ages. It was understood from almost the Tower's earliest days that this custodian would have a right to any livestock that had fallen off a boat into the Thames, or indeed any other unaccounted-for goods in the water. Added to this, there was a tax on boats that brought catches of fish upriver. By the time of the reign of Richard II, this was formalised into an even wider tax on all Thames shipping. It was the requirement that any commercial vessel carrying fish or consignments of wine and rum would have to donate a small portion to the Constable of the Tower before proceeding on their way.

As the centuries rolled by, and traffic upon the river became extraordinarily crowded and busy, this tariff became more and more outdated. And then the opening of the first of the London docks in the eighteenth century, quarter of a mile downriver from the Tower, meant that all that delicious claret and those toothsome oysters were now being diverted elsewhere.

Yet pleasingly, the tax was to transmute into one of the Tower's colourful traditions, upheld by the Royal Navy and its warships. The ceremony involving sailors knocking on the Tower gate, and the Yeoman at first refusing entry before finally admitting them, became firmly set. And now the ceremony of the Constable's Dues underlines the respectful link between the Royal Navy and this Royal Palace, with the barrel of wine forming the centrepiece to a highly civilised lunch at which the wine is sampled by all.

Even more esoteric tipples are to be found at one of the more hidden traditional spaces patronised by the Yeoman Warders: their private pub within the Tower walls. Called 'The Keys' (or more properly 'Yeoman Warders Club'), this tiny establishment is found beneath the battlements to the east of the Tower precincts.

It is only open to the Yeoman Warders, their families and their guests. Once the day's visitors to the Tower have departed, and the Ceremony of the Keys has been performed, off-duty Yeomen Warders have a chance to go and relax in this small bar, with furnishings of rich red leather and somewhat gruesome mementos of the past, such as axes. There is a special Yeoman's ale, served by the pint; but also available is Beefeater Gin. This, of course, leads to what might be one of the most beguiling and imagination-snaring traditions of them all: the idea that the Yeoman Warders still live within the walls of the Tower. There are small houses built into the north-side battlements, decorated with plants and flowers and with little tables outside in the summer. There is even a cosy flat at the top of the Bayward Tower, the bedroom of which used to be a prison cell, and which still has a heavy lock upon the door.

Incidentally, if this sounds like an appealing life, it is worth noting that you need to have served twenty-two years at least in the armed forces to qualify. Additionally, the authorities are looking for candidates not only with a sense of history, but also the ability to relate that history engagingly to countless visitors. In this sense, the job is part military, part performance art. And, in recent years, the authorities have been working hard to increase the diversity of the Beefeaters.

Given that all this is at the centre of the City's roaring, ceaseless 24-hour traffic, one might imagine it to be a noisy place to live, but the reverse is true. The Tower, and its courtyards and its precincts, are startlingly quiet by night, almost as if the stones of time and history are being held within a silent, invisible bubble. It is frequently said that, after hours, and in the early mornings, the Tower and its precincts have the feel of a small village. Everyone knows one another and there are pleasantries exchanged as the day's business gets underway.

One focal point for all Yeoman Warders is one of the Tower's most beguiling traditional features: the ravens. By legend, if they were ever to fly away, the Tower and the nation would fall. The story of how they first came to take up residence in the Tower is slightly less familiar. One account has it that these extraordinarily beautiful, and incredibly noisy, jet-black creatures were first drawn to the fortress in the Middle Ages because of the miasma of blood from executions, which suited their own rather bloodthirsty appetites.

What is certainly true, however, is that the Tower's current ravens are absolutely not vegan. Among the meals they are offered are biscuits soaked in blood (that of small mammals, not humans!). They also greatly favour mice, rat, and raw meat in other forms. Eggs are popular, once a week or so, and sometimes, as a treat, the ravens are fed whole rabbit. Curiously, they enjoy the fur as much as the meat.

Traditionally, there are six ravens. In centuries past, their wings were clipped to prevent them flying away, but these days it is a rather more subtle arrangement involving delicate feather trimming. That way, the ravens still fly around but, rather than travel vast distances, they prefer to see the Tower as home. They have their own special wire aviary on the lawn, just in front of the Bloody Tower, and one of the tasks of the Yeoman Warders is to attend to their needs.

Ravens do not get quite enough credit for their intelligence. They are terrific logical problem solvers and can improvise tools to achieve what they want. But they have other talents too; they are known to have astounding memories, and also the ability to replicate various sounds and noises. All visitors are advised strongly not to feed the birds but, equally, ravens have been known not to turn their beaks up at occasional treats.

The birds mate within the Tower precincts too. Most recently, in 2019, a breeding pair of ravens, Huginn and Muninn, started building a nest. The hatching of the chicks soon followed. The warder chosen to carry the title Ravenmaster and the rest of the Yeoman Warders saw to it that all dietary requirements of the young family were met.

But the story of the ravens across the years was not always quite so tranquil or harmonious. Indeed, it is thought that part of the reason they became so integral to the Tower was precisely because of their Gothic associations. These graveyard birds would provide macabre set-dressing for thrill-seeking tourists. Then there were the ravens that got away . . .

In 1981, one raven – by the name of Grog – flew away from the Tower and made its way into the heart of cockney London, eventually being tracked down to the outside of an old pub called The Rose and Punchbowl. Another managed to get five miles downriver to Greenwich Park, where the vigilance of the public soon had it returned to its home.

The intelligence of ravens generally is a field that is attracting lots of fascinated scientists. Tests have shown that, given tools and treats, with problems to solve using various implements, ravens have performed as skilfully as small children, but with a greater capacity for thinking ahead. One logic conundrum for ravens involved pieces of meat attached to lines of string that were looped around perches in particular sequences, requiring the birds to unravel the loops before they could get at the treats. It was assumed that the ravens would first have to be taught the correct procedure, but as the scientists looked on with some wonder, a number of ravens solved the puzzle unbidden and unaided.

At the Tower, the ravens are sometimes given a cheerful mental workout with a special corvid version of the game KerPlunk, in which short sticks have to be strategically extracted from a tube to prevent a marble falling. In this version, meat is substituted for the marble; and it is supposed to fall. The ravens must work out which sticks to extract to get at it.

The Tower's current Ravenmaster, Yeoman Warder Christopher Skaife, has written a book – aptly titled *The Ravenmaster* – about his feathered charges, and about their complex relationships with each other and, indeed, humans. The seven birds (six is the tradition, but there is a raven kept spare in case of disaster!) have highly distinct personalities, and a rigid hierarchy. They are naturally very wary of humans, but, after some time, they can form bonds with people that last a lifetime. They have a huge range of communication skills: different cries and noises, sometimes straightforward impersonation, and all combined with a mesmeric body language.

They live a surprisingly long time – one of the Tower's most recent ravens died at the age of forty-four – and their habits within the Tower's aviary are sometimes comically rigid. What does seem truly remarkable, and is something you cannot quite believe until you see it close up, is the way that some ravens seem extremely happy to pose for photographs. You might readily see a raven sitting on a waist-high wall outside the Bloody Tower, with visitors arranging themselves next to it, phones held high; the bird itself will angle its head quizzically, and there might be the occasional flutter of a wing. But otherwise it is happy to sit still amid a chattering throng.

Of course, this is another intriguing puzzle, as far as the raven is concerned, that could bring the end result of a treat, and, on these occasions, they try to find the means of persuading the humans to offer titbits. Although, as mentioned, it is very wrong to feed the ravens – their diet is finely balanced – but they have often been witnessed eyeing discarded food eagerly.

So the puzzles in this section pay tribute both to ceremonies and to the creatures who refuse to stand on ceremony. From the logic of keys and locks and security patrols to the intense logical skills of the Tower's feathered mascots, here are headscratchers that illuminate the sides of Tower life that visitors can glimpse, if they are lucky.

1

FIND THE BEEFEATER

Each letter of the alphabet is represented by a number from 1 to 26. We give you the numbers which represent the letters in the word BEEFEATER to start you off below. So every space with a 1 in it contains a B, every space with a 2 contains an E, and so on. The completed grid will be made of words that are written either across or down and interlink as in a conventional crossword.

You might find the checklist below will help to keep track of the letters you have found.

1 = B, 2 = E, 3 = F, 4 = A, 5 =   , 6 =   , 7 =   , 8 =   ,
9 =   , 10 =   , 11 =   , 12 =   , 13 = R, 14 = T,
15 =   , 16 =   , 17 =   , 18 =   , 19 =   , 20 =   ,
21 =   , 22 =   , 23 =   , 24, =   , 25 =   , 26 =   .

When you have filled the crossword and worked out all the letters, look at the numbers below and find the name of a very special Beefeater.

6.21.9.13.4.

15.4.6.2.13.21.17.

21	■	16	■	1	2	2	3	2	4	14	2	13
3	21	9	12	■	7	■	4	■	10	■	2	■
3	■	3	■	8	6	1	13	2	12	12	4	■
11	4	3	4	13	9	■	13	■	5	■	11	■
10	■	2	■	■	10	■	9	■	■	17	■	15
13	8	13	4	12	■	11	15	13	2	2	15	23
9	■	2	■	■	19	4	11	■	■	19	■	2
17	8	17	17	2	13	18	■	11	20	4	13	6
19	■	14	■	■	4	■	26	■	■	14	■	9
■	12	■	11	■	17	■	23	4	1	9	14	11
1	4	11	9	12	9	15	4	■	■	22	■	14
■	22	■	24	■	14	■	26	■	25	2	2	13
15	4	3	2	14	2	13	9	4	■	11	■	18

2

TOWER VISITORS

The Tower welcomes around 17,000 people per day from all over the globe during the summer months. In this puzzle we look at just five individuals who are all at the Tower for a different reason. They visit on a different day of the week and there are five different nationalities.

Look at the information below. When you discover a piece of positive information put a tick in the appropriate box in the grid opposite. Put a cross in any space where there is no link. Keep rereading and recording until you can complete the lower grid.

1   Albert, the guide, is French.

2   The lady who visited on a Monday is there as a tourist. She is not Italian.

3   Charles was there later in the week compared to Eric, who is not a photographer.

4   Brigitte was at the Tower the day before the photographer, who is at the Tower the day before the person from Denmark.

5   The Spanish gentleman was at the Tower on Friday. He is not a teacher.

		DAY					ROLE					NATIONALITY				
		MONDAY	TUESDAY	WEDNESDAY	THURSDAY	FRIDAY	COACH DRIVER	GUIDE	PHOTOGRAPHER	TEACHER	TOURIST	DANISH	ENGLISH	FRENCH	ITALIAN	SPANISH
NAME	ALBERT															
	BRIGITTE															
	CHARLES															
	DENISE															
	ERIC															
NATIONALITY	DANISH															
	ENGLISH															
	FRENCH															
	ITALIAN															
	SPANISH															
ROLE	COACH DRIVER															
	GUIDE															
	PHOTOGRAPHER															
	TEACHER															
	TOURIST															

NAME	DAY	ROLE	NATIONALITY

3

HAND OVER

The Ceremony of the Keys is one of the famous traditions of the Tower as doors are locked and keys handed over.

Suppose that each Yeoman Warder on duty hands over a set of keys to every other Yeoman Warder.

No two Yeoman Warders exchange keys more than once.

In a working roster keys exchange hands fifty-five times.

How many Yeoman Warders were on duty?

4

BACK AND FORTH

The Yeomen Warders of the Tower patrol back and forth in order to protect this ancient building. In the puzzle below the words go back and forth also. The second answer in each pair of clues has the same letters as the first answer but reading backwards, e.g. if the first answer is NIP then the second answer is PIN.

1 Tower of London guard * Make another sketch

2 Part of a castle * Take a sly look

3 Paved area surrounded by buildings * Low cart for beer barrels

4 Exist * Wickedness

5 Grim destiny * State of mind

6 Glide like a river such as the Thames * Pack hunting animal

7 Focus for an astronomer * Rodents

8 Sum offered for the apprehension of a criminal * Storage compartment

5

STARTING WITH THE RAVEN...

Letters in the names of birds have been replaced by symbols. Starting with the RAVEN whose code looks like this:

Using the same code, can you work out the names of the other birds?

1

2

3

4

5

6

6

THE BELL TOWER

The Bell Tower derives its name from the small wooden turret situated on top of the structure which contains the Tower's 'curfew bell'. This was used in the past to inform prisoners who were allowed to walk around the Tower that it was time to return to their quarters. These days it is sounded to inform visitors that the Tower is about to close for the day.

Imagine the unimaginable. A Yeoman Warder has sat down on a bench and nodded off while patrolling the grounds. He is woken by the chime of a bell.

The Yeoman Warder is not carrying a phone and cannot see a clock face.

He knows that the bell chimes on the hour and the number of chimes denotes the hour.

The bell also gives a single chime on every quarter of the hour.

If a single chime woke the Yeoman Warder, what would be the longest period of time he would have to wait before being absolutely certain of what the time was?

7

CEREMONY OF THE KEYS

The Ceremony of the Keys takes place each evening at the Tower and has done so for over seven hundred years. In our puzzle the keys have become a bit mixed up! How many different kinds of keys are hidden here?

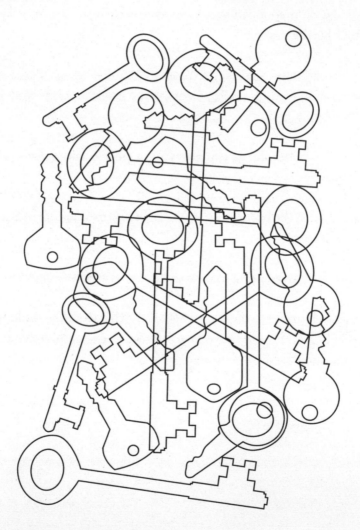

CHAPTER TWELVE

GHOSTS AND ABSOLUTE LEGENDS

THE TOWER'S current Ravenmaster, Christopher Skaife, is a man of steady gaze and firm nerve and practical intelligence, but he, like so many others across the years, has had moments of weird supernatural unease within the Tower's walls.

He has related how he found it increasingly difficult to carry on living in his Tower flat. Although he was reluctant to go into any great detail, he explained how he had become increasingly aware of a presence there. During the night, objects would be moved around. And in the early hours of one morning, he became aware of a figure with him in his room. He requested a transfer to another apartment within the Tower precincts, which was granted. Leaving the question: what happened to the person who inherited that room afterwards?

The story does more than provide a pleasurable frisson of the macabre; it shows that the ghosts of the Tower of London have – in their own curious way – always moved with the times. Stories of spectral disturbance in various sites around the fortress go back centuries, but each of these ghost stories are very distinctive and some are compellingly weird.

Naturally, all historic sites are replete with spectres and some, like Chillingham Castle in Northumberland, are madly competitive about it. After all, nothing lures the paying visitors quite as effectively as the promise of blood-curdling phantoms. But the Tower encompasses all sorts of other legends too, some mythic, some more modern urban legends. From the inscriptions on the walls of prison cells of an astrologic nature to the cat that somehow got down the chimney, from the long-buried head of a Celtic King from thousands of years ago to the earthy reality (and yet legendary status) of the Tower's 1950s prisoners, the Kray twins, there is a dizzying range of legends here. Some are touching, some are hair-raising, others are downright weird.

The tale of the Earl of Southampton's cat continues to bemuse and amuse in equal measure, for instance. In 1601, Henry Wriothesley, Shakespeare's patron, was imprisoned in the Tower after a failed conspiracy against the aged Elizabeth I. Although he was kept in more comfortable quarters than previous luminaries, such as Thomas More, the earl was nonetheless in despair, because the sentence was indeterminate, and it could well have been that he faced the rest of his life there.

Yet one day brought an astonishing and cheering visitation: the appearance of his black-and-white cat, Trixie. According to the story, the cat somehow made its own way across the rooftops of the Tower and thence down a chimney, in order to be by her master's side.

Other versions of the story offer the simpler explanation that the earl's wife, visiting him, brought him the cat as some small means of comfort during his confinement. Whatever the case, the creature ended up immortalised in an oil painting, a portrait of the earl and his cat featuring plenty of Jacobean visual codes, such as a broken windowpane, the earl's long hair worn around his shoulders and his date of imprisonment written in chalk with the release date missing. According to some, these details were clues that might only be read by a receptive monarch and they were aimed directly at the new king, James I, who was susceptible to handsome young men. The broken window was thought to symbolise the violence of the old regime and the imprisonment dates are a direct plea for clemency, with the hair worn long on the shoulders seen as a direct signal of submission to the will of His Majesty. Indeed, the only detail of the painting that seemed not to be a cryptic clue was Trixie the cat.

Leaping forward in time to the grey years following the Second World War, we come across a story that seems as if it ought to be an urban legend and yet was not. Ronnie and Reggie Kray, the notorious twins whose criminal network terrorised London, ended up imprisoned in the Tower even before their life of violent crime got properly started. The year was 1952 and the twins, like all young men, were required to report for eighteen months of National Service with the army. But the twins had other ideas.

The regiment they were supposed to be reporting to, the Royal Fusiliers, noted their failure to materialise, and Ronnie and Reggie were spotted outside an East End pub one day by a police constable, who was under orders to apprehend them. What happened instead was that they beat the policeman up. Eventually they were caught, this time by a larger contingent of constables. It so happened, however, that the Royal Fusiliers had their barracks within the Tower of London.

Thus it was that the violent twins found themselves hauled through those gates like so many before them and locked up, though in rather more utilitarian surrounds than those that had been on offer to the Earl of Southampton. Soon after, they were shipped out to a detention centre in Shepton Mallet, but the army eventually decided that it might manage well enough without their dubious talents (indeed, one of the later objections to the principle of National Service was that it took young criminals and gave them brilliant physical training, which only made them more effective criminals afterwards).

Did the Kray twins make an even more frightening prospect at the Tower than the many ghosts? Indeed, for that matter, did the brief sojourn of Hitler's right-hand man, Rudolf Hess, during the war eclipse any of the creepier presences? Hess had flown out of Germany in 1941 on an eccentric mission and was quickly apprehended in Scotland. From there he was sent by Churchill to the Tower for several days, pending more practical confinement. Indeed, there is a theory that if Hitler had been captured alive in his Berlin bunker in 1945, he would then subsequently have been transported to England

and held in the Tower. Apparently this is why some mock-Victorian windows were fitted to one of the cells near the Queen's House, and also why that cell was upgraded with a modern lavatory to fit prisoner protocols. But among those prisoners who actually were held in the Tower, it is doubtful that even the Kray twins or Hess would be more scary than some of the Tower's ghosts, whose stories have a depth and resonance that go rather beyond figures in white sheets and clanking chains.

The ghost that perhaps might be most expected is that of Anne Boleyn, who is indeed said to stalk Tower Green near the site of her execution, dressed elaborately. This particular ghostly manifestation is perfectly straightforward. One instance of an alleged sighting came in the nineteenth century, when a Yeoman Warder, terrified by the apparition, rather ungallantly ran at her with his dagger. But Anne Boleyn is not the only lady to haunt these grounds, as another prominent aristocratic revenant is said to haunt the Queen's House. Her name is Lady Arbella Stuart, and she was a prisoner in the seventeenth century, jailed after a paranoid James I suspected her of plotting for the throne. She went on hunger strike and subsequently died, though some believed she had been poisoned.

Very slightly more skin-prickling are the stories of the apparitions of the Princes in the Tower. Again, there are accounts that one might expect: that of two boys in medieval clothes, seen either within the Bloody Tower or just outside it, sometimes wringing their hands, sometimes sighing, sometimes vanishing into stone walls. Yet on other occasions the apparitions have been slightly more disquieting. A school party was being taken around the Tower one morning and several small children innocently asked their teacher who the two quiet boys in strange clothes staring at them were.

Then there are the stories that are too weird to be regarded as bait to lure visitors. The White Lady, who is said to haunt the White Tower, has something a little more archetypal about her. She is not a ghost of someone who lived, but a mysterious figure replicated throughout the folklore of the British Isles. This White Lady has been seen at the Tower windows, waving at children below. And, inside the Tower, her presence has been signalled by a sudden overpowering perfume, musty and ancient, together with an oppressive sense of gathering doom.

And ghosts take other forms too. There is the famous tale of the nineteenth-century Yeoman Warder who became aware of a curious fog issuing from beneath a door while on patrol in the small hours of a moonlit night. This fog rose up, and gradually began to assume a shape. As the shape solidified, the Warder could see it was that of a vast bear, with unfathomably dark eyes. It is tempting to think of this as the ghost of the medieval polar bear, kept in the menagerie and fishing in the Thames on a leash.

Markedly more malevolent is the dark presence in the Armoury. Across the years, Yeoman Warders have testified to a frightening phenomenon that is said to happen close to Henry VIII's suit of armour, and again in the silence of the night, when patrols are undertaken. The story goes that it first feels as if some invisible presence has dropped from the ceiling. What then follows is a sensation of crushing, of having one's torso squeezed unbearably by some terrible, massive grip. Another version of the story had a Yeoman Warder, alone in the echoing room, suddenly held immobile by the sense of his neck being gripped from behind, as though he was being garrotted with fabric. Later, he found he had bruising on his neck from the intensity of the attack.

The most curious and surreal story was relayed by a former Keeper of the Crown Jewels, Edmund Lenthal Swifte, who saw a manifestation one night in 1817. He and his family occupied a cosy apartment at the top of the Jewel House, which he noted had once been the 'doleful' residence of Anne Boleyn. What happened that October night, however, bore no relation to her. The sitting room, he attested, was 'irregularly shaped', with a large chimneypiece, two windows and three doors. To stave off the chills of an autumn evening, the 'doors were closed' and 'heavy and dark cloth curtains' hung down from the windows. Swifte was there with his son, his wife and his sister-in-law.

He had passed a glass of 'wine and water' to his wife, who, upon raising it to her lips, suddenly looked up and exclaimed, 'Good God! What is that?'

The uncanny and curious apparition was a cylinder, 'like a glass tube', 'the thickness of an arm', and it proceeded to float between the dining table and the ceiling. This cylinder appeared to contain a dense, azure fluid, which 'rolled' and 'mingled' incessantly within. Swifte and his wife watched it in silence for about two minutes and then the cylinder began to move. It floated towards Swifte's sister-in-law and then, moving along the table, it floated in front of his son and Swifte himself before moving towards his wife. It moved behind her, and came to a halt, hovering over her right shoulder. Without turning, Swifte's wife exclaimed: 'Oh Christ! It has seized me!' She crouched down, clasping her shoulders, and Swifte, in what sounds like a fugue state of terror, leapt from his chair, ran from the room and up the stairs to his smaller children, there with their nurse, and gabbled what he had seen.

Yet there was an even more curious twist: only Swifte and his wife had actually seen the cylinder. His son, sitting at the table, and his sister-in-law, one chair along, had seen nothing.

And what was to be made of it? The next day, Swifte consulted with the Tower's chaplain, but the chaplain could offer no form of explanation or comfort. Nothing like this had been seen before, but others in the precincts were reminded of old stories of necromancy, when young women in the Tower some years back had been 'suspected of making phantasmagorical experiments'.

If ghosts are a form of distorted historical tribute, then perhaps the most moving account of a haunting involved a Yeoman Warder in the 1860s, who was passing Tower Green on a dark and quiet night when he saw lights from the windows of the Chapel of St Peter ad Vincula. Apprehensive, but also mindful of not wanting to walk in on some sacred service that he had not been informed of, he carefully made his way to the windows and looked within.

Bathed in a beautiful glowing iridescence, he saw a procession of dead nobles and notaries moving down the aisle of the chapel, led by Anne Boleyn (a ubiquitous supernatural fixture), with her face turned away. As the Yeoman Warder watched, the figures walked on and disappeared. It was as though they were laying eternal claim to the chapel. When one considers the range of figures whose remains can still be found there, from Anne Boleyn to Thomas More and Thomas Cromwell, there is something rather poignant about a tale involving their dignified spirits somehow finding a form of peace with one another.

But the Tower has even greater claim to eternity than that, for the site is also one of Celtic and Druidic significance. The fortress is built upon what some term the 'White Hill'. And there was a time when, buried beneath that hill, was the most extraordinary secret: a talisman from an infinitely older religion than Christianity, set in place to protect the land and its people. This talisman was the head of a giant who had once been a leader of men.

The story of Bran the Blessed – Bran is Welsh for raven – first found written form in the thirteenth century in the Welsh mythic epic collection of tales *The Mabinogion*, which were themselves part of a much more venerable oral tradition. Bran was a giant who used his own body to form a bridge across the sea to the realm of Ireland, allowing his armies and people to walk over his back, but, in the course of some extraordinary battles and betrayals, he was mortally wounded by a poisoned dart shot into his foot. He had a curious request for his loyal lieutenants, as he lay dying: he asked them to cut off his head, and to bear it safely back across the sea. This they did, and Bran's head continued to talk to them happily as they all journeyed back east.

But it was now time to find the most suitable place to inter this head of power. Preferably a site where he would be both facing the water and facing the threatening lands across the sea. And according to some versions of the legend, Bran's head was buried at the site where the south east of the Tower of London looks out over Tower Bridge. This was the base of the White Hill: a propitious spot.

There was a further legend, too, that came down the generations, and related directly to this mighty giant, about another extraordinary leader, a king whose mission was to unite and protect the realm. This king, knowing of the secret resting place of the head of Bran, had it removed from the earth. This usurping figure was the equally mythic Arthur, who wished it to be known that it was he, and not Bran, keeping the realm safe and whole.

Naturally, there are those who have made the delightful folkloric connection between Bran and the birds that share his (Welsh) name. Even if his head is no longer there, the ravens continue his work, some feel, with their presence ensuring that the realm does not fall.

The legends of Tower Hill don't stop here, mind you. Before the Conqueror, there was apparently a spring which produced clear and effervescent water, which was supposed to have marvellous healing effects. And Bran was not the only mythological figure to have been buried on the hill, because, according to folklore, it was also the last resting place of London's original founder, Brutus. Brutus had come to Britain when he fled from Troy, a thousand years before the birth of Christ. He was a prince, who was beckoned towards the site by a vision of the goddess Diana.

This man of Troy immediately had to face two monstrous giants right near the site of the Tower-to-be, called Gog and Magog. After defeating them in battle, Brutus was now free to establish a new city by the waters of the Thames. This was to be a New Troy. And, indeed, this was the story told by the pioneering historian monk Geoffrey of Monmouth, around 1135, and it was a legend so seductive that it came to be believed by succeeding generations of Plantagenets and Tudors. Curiously, it is also, in essence, an origin story based upon invasion, and one which showed an invasion as having brought nothing but good to the land. In that sense, Geoffrey of Monmouth might also have been quietly suggesting that William the Conqueror – of recent memory, at that time – was also an invader who brought the blessing of innovation and strength.

In the eighteenth century, a fresh incarnation of Druidic enthusiasm brought Brutus's name back to the fore among esoteric followers, and the Tower of London came to be associated with this ancient power and wisdom. And now, each spring equinox, the area just outside the walls of the Tower plays host to a charming and (for some) rather moving ceremony.

Each year, Druids gather here, white-robed and solemn, to mark the coming of the spring. In one account, the Tower of London is aligned with the equinox dawn sunrise. There is a brief horn recital and then a contemplative silence. As well as being a pleasing contrast to the general soulless thrum of the City of London, the ceremony also tangentially serves to make visitors and Londoners alike look afresh at the Tower, and to appreciate its age.

So the puzzles in this final chapter will carry that charge of the other-worldly, and the sense of the vast space of time. Here too are puzzles on the timings of ghosts' nocturnal glidings, puzzles deciphering etched wall messages, or seeking out long buried artefacts, and even teasers about how pet cats might find ingenious and extraordinary routes in and out of the Tower.

1

BEHEADING

Examples of beheading are sadly legendary in the history of the Tower. In this puzzle, we look at 'beheading' of a very different kind.

Look at the clues on the opposite page. When you have found the answer, you must 'behead' it, i.e. take off the first letter to create a new word. The new word is then fitted into the grid below.

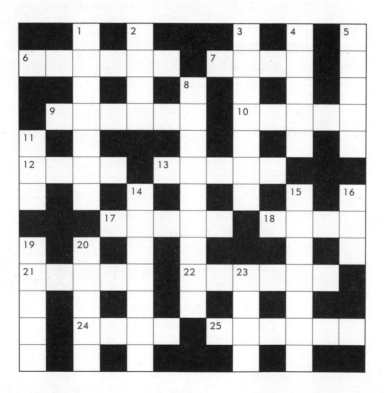

ACROSS

6 Remote Russian republic

7 Woodwind instrument

9 Complain

10 Games

12 Specific type of animal such as a dog

13 Very thin slice

17 Spade

18 Deceive, fail to play by the rules

21 Delivered a blow

22 Narrow water channels

24 Divide fairly

25 Acquired information

DOWN

1 Took for granted

2 Make an ascent

3 Having the right kit

4 Large clippers or scissors

5 Stew in the oven

8 Leaders of republics

11 Outer casing of a tree

14 Cups, saucers, plates, etc.

15 Assisting in something illegal

16 After the appointed time

19 Parent

20 Purchased

23 Polite form of address to a woman

2

TURN OF THE SCREW

Tales of thumbscrews and the rack abound in the catalogue of dark deeds at the Tower.

Here's a sketch of four cog wheels forming a mesh as part of some despicable device. All the wheels have a number of teeth, as indicated on the wheels.

The device is started.

How many times will the large cog wheel have to turn before ALL wheels return to their starting position?

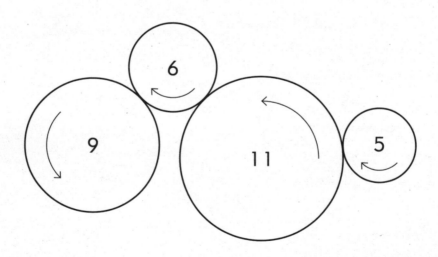

3

DICEY

Some prisoners were kept imprisoned in the Tower for a long time.

The playing of dice was one of the things that many gaolers did to pass the hours. Usually they played the game among themselves and sometimes with the prisoners. Some gaolers found there were some rich pickings to be earned from their high-born charges.

Not everyone played by the rules. On a standard six-sided dice the two opposite sides always add up to seven. This is a decidedly dodgy dice, that was doubtless used in a game of skulduggery.

Here are three views of the dice.

How many dots appear on the opposite side to the two dots as shown on dice B?

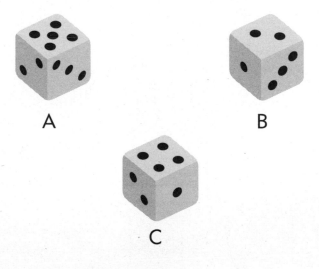

A   B

C

4
EXIT ROUTE

Lady Bird is imprisoned in a dark place in the Tower, and is becoming desperate to find a means of escape. Scrawled on the walls of her prison there are groups of straight lines which draw her attention. Could they be her escape route? Has someone taken this journey before and tasted freedom again? It's a chance she must take. Through which parts of the Tower does she make her escape?

5

SKULLDUGGERY

Here's a maze of underground tunnels. You want to find a route that takes you past the least number of skulls possible. The escape route will lead you to which of the three named towers?

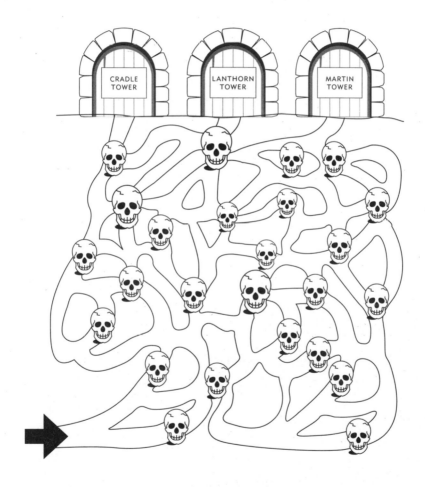

6

NOW YOU SEE IT ...

Look at the groups of letters below. Like a ghost hunter you are looking for something that you can't see! Try to find a word within each group so that completed words appear before your very eyes. All the invisible words have a ghostly or Tower link.

1   E F _ _ _ _ L E S S
COM _ _ _ _ A B L E
_ _ _ _ U N A T E

2   M I D _ _ _ _ _
K _ _ _ _ _
_ _ _ _ _ M A R E

3   _ _ _ N D A
P A S S _ _ _ W A Y
S A U S _ _ _ S

4   _ _ _ _ O W S
D U M B _ _ _ _ S
R E _ _ _ _ I O N

5   _ _ _ _ _ L I H O O D
S _ _ _ _ R
D E _ _ _ _ R Y

7

STARE-WELL

It is hard to imagine the feelings of those who descended the steps to the dungeons of the Tower, wondering if they would ever see the outside world again. Stare hard at the stairwell below. Focus on the stairwell. Move the page around. Are the stairs going up, or are the stairs going down? You decide!

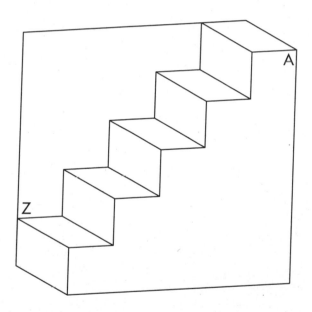

CONCLUSION

IN THE autumn of 2014, an extraordinary wave of scarlet filled the moat, covering the green grass, and made the Tower of London a beautiful site of mourning. The inspired idea was an art installation entitled *Blood Swept Lands and Seas Of Red*, and it took the form of 888,246 painstakingly made ceramic poppies. The purpose was to mark the hundredth anniversary since the start of the First World War. Like all great art, it became something very much larger than itself and gave the Tower a new role as a focus for remembrance.

The artists were Paul Cummins and Tom Piper. Each of the poppies that they made were intended to symbolise a British military fatality during the course of the 'Great War'. The unforgettable brilliance rested not merely on the breathtaking scale of the project, but on the ingenious ways in which the architecture of the Tower of London was used to maximise the impact.

At the northern side of the Tower, one of the openings in the rampart wall overlooking the moat became known as the 'Weeping Window', for, when viewed from a distance, it appeared that the poppies were pouring out from within, down the wall and pooling in the moat below, creating a great mass of red. On the south side, facing the river, poppies appeared to form a jet, arching over the rampart wall, to fall into the space beneath. In reality, the ceramic poppies were held together with wires. But the sanguinary effect was mesmerising and visitors started to come simply to behold the display and think about its sombre meanings.

In the rich ruby sunsets of the autumn that effect was deepened and, at each sundown, the names of one hundred and eighty Commonwealth military casualties were read out from a roll of honour. These names could be nominated by members of the public, who wanted their own distant family members to be commemorated. It was estimated that some five million people came from all corners of the world to take part in this unique festival of remembrance.

More recently, the centenary of the end of the war was marked by filling the vast wide moat with candlelight. These lights represented the lives of those who had fallen. And each evening, as with the poppies, there was a special ceremony to pay tribute.

So, despite its very great age, the Tower of London continually evolves as a focal point for Londoners and for visitors. It remains, in the eyes of the world, a perfect symbol of Britishness: ancient yet modern, formal yet incredibly quirky, dignified yet eccentric, packed with royal treasure yet open to all. It is to be hoped that all these puzzles have helped spark ever more appreciation of this fortress. The layers of history are woven together with all those bizarre stories, from Elizabeth I furiously sitting in the water beneath Traitor's Gate to the ingenious and madcap escapes, from Oliver Cromwell melting down centuries, worth of Crown Jewels to Sir Walter Raleigh's herbal garden. For here is a world that ought to be about pageantry yet ends up being much more about humanity.

Just as we try to imagine what it must have been like to be the young Lady Jane Grey, or Anne Boleyn, or even Thomas More or Thomas Cromwell – the cold shadow of the axeman drawing closer – so too we think of the less familiar and rather more cheerfully colourful aspects of life within the Tower, from the elaborate designs of those Plantagenet wallhangings to the abstruse chemical experiments carried out by the Earl of Northumberland and his resident mathematicians.

The Tower itself is a puzzle, for how can one fortress hold within it the patterns of so many centuries? The layout is the most delightful maze, with the spiral staircase of the White Tower leading out on to the narrow Norman arched corridor that in turn leads to the unexpected splendour of the Chapel of St John, which looks too big to fit within that corner of the building. Then there are the chambers of Edward I in the Wakefield Tower, which lead to seemingly never-ending steps that go up and down, and twist and turn, until you suddenly find yourself within a throne room and an adjacent chapel in quite a different tower.

To move around this fortress is to be catapulted back and forth across the centuries. In one short visit you can see eleventh-century Norman fireplaces, fourteenth-century bedclothes, sixteenth-century hexagonal stone cells and ponderous Victorian pastiches of jewel stores, with each of these layers of time carrying a charge of enigma and mystery. But the Yeoman Warders, experts in the field of Tower history, are always there to unlock and illuminate those age-old puzzles. No question that you could ever put to them will elicit a scratched head. And it is extraordinary to think that Henry VIII, if he could somehow be resurrected, would look upon today's Yeoman Warders and around the precincts they guard, and marvel at just how little had changed across the space of five hundred years. In the Tower, time has moved at a different speed – and that is its most enjoyable puzzle of all.

1

QUIZ CROSSWORD

Test yourself on how much you have remembered about the Tower with our quiz crossword.

ACROSS

7 The Tower was famously a fortress, a prison and what else? (6)

9 Which Cromwell ordered that the Crown Jewels be melted down after the execution of Charles I? (6)

10 What honour has been bestowed on a man with the title 'Sir'? (10)

11 Before she became the monarch Princess Elizabeth was a prisoner in the Tower. Legend gives her the title Good and which nickname? (4)

12 What name is given to the metal and ribbon award given to a soldier? (5)

13 Which first name was shared by three of Henry VIII's wives? (9)

16 When a monarch receives the ceremonial headdress for the first time they are said to be what? (7)

21 What name is given to those who act treacherously and are disloyal to their country? (9)

22 Two of Henry VIII's children grew up to take on which role? (5)

24 (& 15 Down) Which sixteen-year-old Lady reigned for just nine days? (4,4)

25 What is the popular nickname for 8 Down? (10)

26 A gauntlet, a helmet and a breastplate are all types of what? (6)

27 Which Robert, Earl of Leicester, was a favourite of Elizabeth I? (6)

DOWN

1 If a ghost walks abroad, a place is said to be what? (7)

2 What was the name of an executioner whose deadly weapon was a rope? (7)

3 What is another name for a landing pier, such as that by the notorious Traitor's Gate? (5)

4 The first sovereign minted at the Tower in 1489 was made from what? (4)

5 Which librettist co-wrote an operetta about the Tower? (7)

6 What name was given to one of the group, led by Wat Tyler, who stormed the Tower in 1381? (7)

8 Who famously guard the Tower in their distinctive blue 'undress', or red 'full State' uniforms? (6,7)

14 Where on a boot is a spur attached? (4)

15 See 24 Across

17 Which word means to wed again? Henry VIII did this five times! (7)

18 What is another word for liberty, which many Tower prisoners went to extraordinary lengths to regain? (7)

19 What is the situation where a person is arrested and held before trial and sentencing? (7)

20 Which word might describe the scholar and Lord Chancellor Sir Thomas More who was an expert in law? (7)

23 What appeared on the sides of coins and were famously lost by Walter Raleigh, Anne Boleyn, Thomas Cromwell and many more? (5)

25 Which word can mean to hide treasure in the ground or inter a body? (4)

2

TOWER TEASERS

A selection of brainteasers based on this much-loved London landmark.

a) Terry and Poppy are working their way through some questionnaires completed by visitors to the Tower. 'That's odd,' thought Poppy as she was keying in the answers, 'the occupations of these visitors have something in common.' Look at these occupations and work out Poppy's line of thought. The occupations were:

POET, PORTER, POTTER, PRIOR, REP, RETIREE, TUTOR, WRITER.

b) ANNE, AVA, ENA, ERN, EVA, RENE and VERA are regular visitors to the Tower. They share a favourite element of the Tower of London. What is it, and why?

c) Yeoman Warder Martin has some very precise habits. The middle child in his family, he used to be a police constable, but never became a sergeant. He puts salt on his food but never pepper. He eats sandwiches made from white bread, never brown or wholemeal. He owns a house made of brick, with some flint, but no stone to be seen. The front door has a bell not a door knocker. Water is pumped from a well, rather than from the mains. A keen DIY enthusiast, he has built a wardrobe for every bedroom, preferring this to making chests of drawers. How do you account for Yeoman Warder Martin's behaviour?

FURTHER READING

The Tower of London in the History of the Nation, A. L. Rowse (Weidenfeld & Nicolson, 1972)

Tower: An Epic History of the Tower of London, Nigel Jones (Hutchinson, 2011)

Foundation: The History of England Volume I, Peter Ackroyd (Macmillan, 2011)

The Isles: A History, Norman Davies (Macmillan, 1999)

Richard III and *Henry VI, Part III*, collected in the magisterial *The Oxford Shakespeare: The Complete Works* (Second Edition), edited by Stanley Wells and others (Oxford University Press, 2005)

ANSWERS

CHAPTER ONE

TOWERING OVER ALL

1

FROM THE FORTRESS

Efts, Errs, Fore, Forest, Fort, Forte, Fosse, Foster, Fret, Frost, Ores, Resort, Rest, Retro, Roster, Rote, Rots, Serf, Sets, Soft, Softer, Sore, Sorest, Sort, Sorter, Store, Toes, Tore, Tort, Torte, Toss, Tress. If you think you have any more legitimate words, then good for you, but don't write in and tell us!

2

CAEN BLOCKS

KEYS cannot be used. The three blocks are:

CAEN ABLE ELMS NEST.

ACRE CAEN READ ENDS.

DISC IOTA STYE CAEN.

3

TARGET PRACTICE

1 Castle, **2** Arrest, **3** Bloody, **4** Dagger,
5 Beaten, **6** Escape, **7** Patrol, **8** Ravens,
9 Fought, **10** Battle, **11** Sentry, **12** Bronze.

4

RECTANGLED

51

5

WORK IN PROGRESS

25

6

ARCHWAY REPAIRS

1 and 6, 2 and 9, 3 and 4, 5 and 8, 7 and 10.

CHAPTER TWO

DARING ESCAPES AND CRUEL CAGES

1

KEEP SAFE

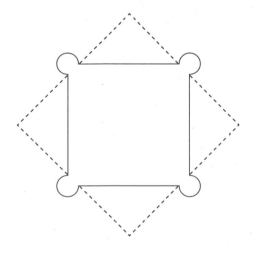

2

BOATMEN

Seven boats leaving is the maximum before a break. The pattern is: downstream, downstream, upstream, upstream, upstream, downstream, downstream.

3

ALL CHANGE

Grid A: Crown, Frown, Flown, Flows, Flaws, Flags.

Grid B: Track, Trick, Trice, Trite, Write, White.

4

TOWER TRAIL

The trail begins with the DEVEREUX tower and continues with LANTHORN, WARDROBE, WAKEFIELD, BEAUCHAMP, BROAD ARROW, CONSTABLE, DEVELIN, BOWYER, BLOODY, WHITE, WELL, BYWARD, MIDDLE, MARTIN, FLINT, BELL, SALT.

5

ON REFLECTION

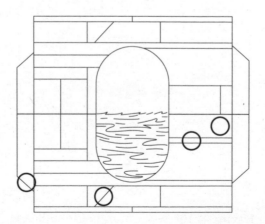

6

ESCAPES AND RECAPTURE

1 Enlighten, **2** Terminate, **3** Keepsake, **4** Emblem,
5 Heartache, **6** Steadfast, **7** Thousandth, **8** Neckline.

7

LINES OF DEFENCE

C8, I3 and G5.

CHAPTER THREE

THE ZOO IN THE TOWER

1

FAVOURITES

Anne went on a Wednesday and liked the Polar Bear.

Catherine went on a Monday and liked the Lion.

Henry went on a Tuesday and liked the Elephant.

Thomas went on a Thursday and liked the Baboon.

2

ESCAPED

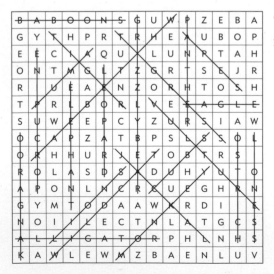

The ZEBRA cannot be found. It has escaped!

3

PENNED IN

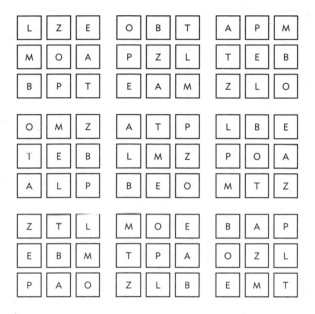

4

HIDDEN ANIMALS

1 Bear, **2** Zebra, **3** Jackal,
4 Monkey, **5** Ostriches, **6** Ape.

5

TWO ZOOS

6

ONE EXTRA

Three cages are involved. The movement can work involving any corner cage, plus the two adjacent cages. Let's take the cage where corridor A and corridor C meet. Move one animal from the corner cage to the middle cage of A. Move another animal from the corner cage to the middle cage of C. A now lines up with an enclosure of five (which has not changed), the middle with six and corner A/C with three. In corridor C, the corner C/D still houses five animals, the centre area now has six animals, and corner A/C contains three. Both A and C have fourteen creatures on show. Introduce the new animal in to A/C. Now both corridors contain fifteen animals.

7

BEAR PAIR

2 and 5 are identical.

Look at the neck and head in 1, the left paw in 3, the left ear in 4 and the manacle in 6.

CHAPTER FOUR

KA-BOOM!

1
CHAIN MAIL

HELMET is unused. Chain, Letter, Box, Office, Block, Capital, City, Centre, Stage, Coach, Party, Line, Dance, Hall, Stand, Off, Side, Board, Meeting, House, Fly, Half, Penny, Black, Mail.

2
JOUSTING

90 yards. When the two knights meet for the second time they will have covered three times the length of the track between them. The Black Knight covered 37 yards at the first meeting. He will now have travelled three times that distance, which is 111 yards. He has completed 21 yards of his second charge. Take that number away from the total distance he has travelled to reveal the length of the jousting track. $111 - 21 = 90$ yards.

3

BULL'S-EYE

Eight arrows are needed. The temptation is to start with higher numbers, but the answer is to look at the smaller numbers. Six arrows in circle worth 13 (= 78) + two arrows in circle worth 11 (= 22) will do it (78 + 22 = 100).

4

ARMOURY AWRY

1 Grenade, **2** Sabre, **3** Lance, **4** Rifle, **5** Gun, **6** Pike, **7** Spear, **8** Pistol, **9** Dagger, **10** Missile.

5

LOITERING WITHIN TENT

Shape C

6

READY FOR BATTLE

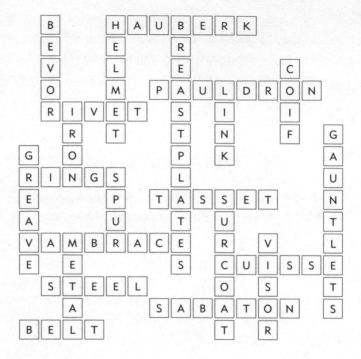

7

UNDER SIEGE

The Deadliest (D), the Hardiest (H) and the Kingsfollowers (K) will meet at location 8.

CHAPTER FIVE

THE SHADOW OF THE AXEMAN

1

WORD PLAY

THE TOWER warders were looking for THE escaped FELON but HE was NOWHERE to be seen. WHERE was HE? Had HE FOOLED them this time? HE had a secret LETTER for THE heir to the THRONE, and if its secrets WERE revealed they all could be in danger. Had HE already THROWN it away or buried it in a FLOWER bed? THE THREE warders, Thomas, Richard and Henry began to WONDER if the ROTTEN criminal was hiding HERE near TOWER Green. Surely it was WORTH another look!

2

IN DISGUISE

Across: 7 Arches, 8 Heroic, 10 Treason, 11 Spear, 12 Each, 13 Never, 17 Forts, 18 Free, 22 Traps, 23 Avenger, 24 Gaoler, 25 Saddle.

Down: 1 Battles, 2 Screech, 3 Beast, 4 Feasted, 5 Tower, 6 Scare, 9 Ancestral, 14 Monster, 15 Tragedy, 16 Rearmed, 19 Stage, 20 Manor, 21 Regal.

3

OUT OF THE SHADOWS

1 Avarice, **2** Non-stop, **3** Nod, Try, **4** Epistle, **5** Beehive,
6 Organic, **7** Leveret, **8** Ejected, **9** Yew, Oak, **10** Natural.

The 'doomed soul' is Anne Boleyn, second wife of Henry VIII, and
the quotation completes her final words, 'I heard say the executioner
was very good; and I have a little neck.'

4

SINISTER SILHOUETTES

Silhoutte A is an exact match. In B, the space between the man's leg
and the block is filled in. In C, the axe blade is completely smooth.

5

GUARD DUTY

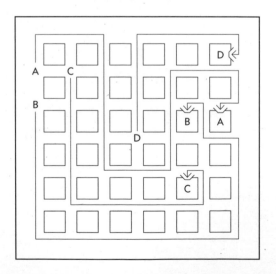

6

BROKEN BONES

1 Car, Pen, Try – Carpentry, **2** Con, Son, Ant – Consonant,
3 For, Bid, Den – Forbidden, **4** Pat, Ron, Age – Patronage,
5 Red, Eve, Lop – Redevelop, **6** Sub, Jug, Ate – Subjugate,
7 Sun, Bat, Her – Sunbather, **8** The, Ref, Ore – Therefore.

7

VOWEL PLAY

1 Thomas More, **2** Anne Boleyn, **3** Catherine Howard,
4 Thomas Culpepper, **5** Lady Jane Grey, **6** Thomas Cromwell,
7 Sir Walter Raleigh, **8** Guy Fawkes.

CHAPTER SIX

MAKING A MINT

1

COINING IT

Thomas started with 21 coins. The amount was doubled to 42. 24 coins were spent, leaving 18.

The butcher counted 18 coins, and added 18 of his own to make 36. 24 coins were spent, leaving 12. The merchant counted 12 coins and added 12 of his own to make 24. 24 coins were spent, leaving Thomas with no coins.

2

PENNY WISE

Andrea saved 28 coins. Bill saved 496 coins. Charles saved 4,186 coins. Daisy saved 67,161 coins. 2000 was a leap year and February had 29 days in it rather than the usual 28. The year had a total of 366 days, instead of the usual 365 days.

3

HEADS OR TAILS?

1 Cocktail, **2** Retail, **3** Headhunt, **4** Detail, **5** Headroom,
6 Headline, **7** Curtail, **8** Entail, **9** Headstrong, **10** Headquarters.

4

POINTER

Three moves. The bottom coin is moved to above the centre of the original top row. The two coins that were on the ends of the original top are added to the two coins now forming the new bottom row. The triangle now points towards the north.

5

COIN COLLECTION

301

6

MINT STREET

1 Sovereign, **2** Bob, **3** Pound, **4** Guinea,
5 Penny, **6** Tanner, **7** Crown, **8** Half crown.

7

SPOT THE FAKES

There are five genuine coins and three fakes. The fakes are coins C, D and G. C has the 1 reversed at the foot of coin. D has the middle horizontal stroke taken from the letter E in PENNY. G has one whole horizontal bar removed from the portcullis symbol.

CHAPTER SEVEN

THE WIZARD AND THE SCHOOL OF NIGHT

1

THE CANNONBALL CONUNDRUMS

Cannonball Conundrum 1: 25.
Cannonball Conundrum 2: 6.
Cannonball Conundrum 3: Hexagons.

2

THE CHALLENGE OF TRAJECTORY

Harriot's trajectory calculation was skewed by one thing: he assumed that heavy objects always fell much faster than lighter objects, without taking into account velocity, mass and air resistance and how they impact on both an arrow and a cannonball.

3

THE RIDDLES OF THE TOWER

Poem 1: Sir Walter's advice is to behave or one day you might find yourself facing the hangman! The wood is the timber of the gallows, the weed is the rope that forms the noose, or 'hangman's bag', and the wag is the son.

Poem 2: The first fourteen lines are a brilliantly comic over-dramatisation of a game of cards that goes on deep into the night, represented by 'four kings' in 'tumult', men suffering 'great losses' and the 'dead bones' 'tumbling' up and down which may be the dice. Then there is the enigma of the 'herald' in the last two lines: what is this unearthly creature that brings the peace? It is in fact a cockerel, announcing that dawn has broken.

Poem 3: This word that 'changeth not' even when 'turned around' or split in two is Anna. And there is sinister historical resonance when one considers the contemporary rumour of Wyatt's affair with Anne Boleyn . . .

Poem 4: The gift Thomas Wyatt describes is a kiss. In a #MeToo age, this solution does not wear too well.

4

THE REBELLIOUS CIPHERS

The key to the code is that letters and numbers alternate; and they run backwards through the alphabet. Z = A, Y = 1, X = B, W = 2, V = C, U = 3 until you reach B = M and A = 13.

Cryptic Code 1: *Myself with ten gentlemen and a hundred of our followers will undertake the delivery of your royal person from the hands of your enemies.*

Cryptic Code 2: *There be six noble gentlemen, all my private friends, who for the zeal they bear to the Catholic cause and your Majesty's service will undertake that tragical execution.*

CHAPTER EIGHT

ALL THAT GLITTERS

1

DIAMOND DISCOVERY

Across: 2 Pie, 4 Delve, 6 Bravely, 8 Cry, 9 Fed, 11 Too, 12 Aim, 14 Seated, 15 Forgot, 16 Ash, 18 Nip, 19 Ten, 21 Bet, 22 Resided, 25 Waved, 26 Pen.

Down: 1 Silver, 2 Pea, 3 Eve, 4 Dry, 5 Elf, 6 Brother, 7 Yearned, 8 Coast, 10 Digit, 11 Tea, 13 Mop, 17 Quiver, 20 New, 21 Bed, 23 Sap, 24 Den.

Shaded word: CULLINAN.

2

A PAIR OF RINGS

Ring 1: 1 Angel, 2 Elope, 3 Peach, 4 Chime, 5 Mecca, 6 Cacti, 7 TIARA, 8 Range, 9 Geese, 10 Sedan.

Ring 2: 1 Never, 2 Erode, 3 Deuce, 4 Cello, 5 Lotto, 6 TOPAZ, 7 Azure, 8 Rebus, 9 Usual, 10 Alone.

3

SYMBOLS

1 Opal, **2** Pearl, **3** Emerald, **4** Sapphire, **5** Diamond.

4

CORONATION QUIZ

1 1902 and 1911 (Edward VII and George V), **2** The 1937 Coronation of George VI, **3** Edward VII who was crowned in 1902. The other Coronations were 1911, 1937 and 1953 (Elizabeth II.)

5

THE JEWEL HOUSE

Anne is third in the queue. She is impressed by the Imperial State Crown as she particularly likes diamonds. Elizabeth is first in the queue. She prefers the Orb. Her name begins with E as does her favourite jewel the emerald. Kate was second to step on to the walkway. She likes the Ampulla. Rubies are her favourite stone. Philip was fourth in the queue. He was amazed by the magnificence of the Sceptre and likes sapphires. William was the final visitor of the group. His favourite was the St Edward's Crown and he especially likes pearls.

6

CROWN MAKING

There were 105 jewels. The 49 sapphires were $^{7}/_{15}$ of the total as the rubies and emeralds together would be $^{8}/_{15}$. $^{1}/_{15}$ would be 7 jewels, therefore 100% ($^{15}/_{15}$) would be 105.

CHAPTER NINE

STAR CHARTS AND MYSTERIOUS SYMBOLS

1

STAR CROSSED

The words are: PHYSICS, COMPASS, ANALYSE, NITRATE, THEOREM, CHEMIST, SAMPLES.

Put them in the order: COMPASS, CHEMIST, ANALYSE, NITRATE, SAMPLES, THEOREM, PHYSICS and the diagonal will read CHARLES. Charles II appointed the first Astronomer Royal, John Flamsteed.

2

IN ORBIT

It will take four years. Planet X will have completed two orbits. Planet Y will have completed one orbit. Both planets will be in position as pictured. Planet Z will have completed half of its full orbit, but all three planets will be in line with the Sun.

3

PARCHMENT PUZZLE

Parchments 2, 3 and 5 are the same.

4

SYMBOLIC

Shape 3. The symbols each contain a letter. Turn the page a quarter to the right to see all the shapes. Starting with Z and working backwards in alphabetical order, the symbols contain a Z, Y, X and W. You are looking for a shape containing a letter V.

5

THE YEAR IN QUESTION

White star = 1, Shaded planet = 2, Black planet = 3, White planet = 4, Cosmic cloud = 5, Ringed panet = 6 and Black star = 7.

The year in question is 1675, the year the first Astronomer Royal, Sir John Flamsteed, was allowed the use of the White Tower as an Observatory.

CHAPTER TEN

A TOUCH OF LUXURY

1

QUIZ QUOTE

1 Jailers, **2** Archery, **3** Chapels, **4** Kingdom, **5** Panther,
6 Outlaws, **7** Ireland, **8** Normans, **9** Trumpet.

The character, Jack Point, from Gilbert & Sullivan's 'The Yeomen of
the Guard' says, 'There is humour in all things.'

2

WORD TOWER

(reading from the top down)
PLACATE, PALACE, PLACE, LACE, ACE, RACE,
REACH, PREACH, CHAPTER.

The shaded letters will spell out the word CHAPEL. The Tower has
two, St John and St Peter ad Vincula.

3

HERALDIC COLOURS

1 Red, **2** Blue, **3** Gold, **4** Black, **5** Green,
6 Silver, **7** Rose, **8** Purple.

4

FAMILY CREST

Shield 6 is the correct one. Shield 1 does contain a triangle. Shield 2 contains a triangle and has the bird facing to his left. Shield 3 has more white than black squares. Shield 4 has an even number of swords. Shield 5 contains a triangle. Shield 7 has the bird facing to his left. Shield 8 has the sword pointing outwards. Shield 9 has an even number of swords.

5

CHEERS

B, C, E, A, G, D, F. Each Lord identified three wines correctly, making a total of nine right answers. Every wine has been correctly named at least once, so that takes up seven of the right answers. No wine got everyone's vote, so there must be two wines that two people agreed on. (five wines identified once + two wines identified twice = nine right answers.)

B as first, and C as second can now be placed. Given that B and C appear as the third wines to be served, the only remaining option – wine E – has to be correct. No Lord identified more than three wines, and Lord Rouge has already done that. All his subsequent answers have to be wrong. Process of elimination places the final four wines in order.

6

FOOD SHARE

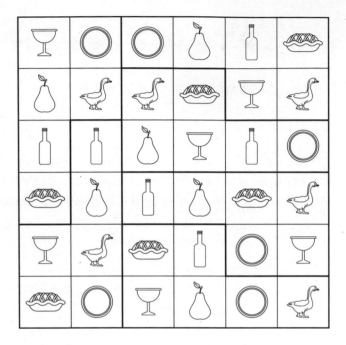

7

MEDIEVAL BANQUET

1 Swan, **2** Pheasant, **3** Wild boar, **4** Partridge, **5** Venison,
6 Cloves, **7** Ginger, **8** Cardamom, **9** Saffron, **10** Nutmeg.

CHAPTER ELEVEN

CEREMONIES AND RAVENS

1

FIND THE BEEFEATER

Across left to right top to bottom: Beefeater, Foil, Umbrella, Safari, Rural, Screech, Gas, Nunnery, Swarm, Habits, Basilica, Jeer, Cafeteria.

Down left to right top to bottom: Offspring, Different, Equip, Fabrics, Apex, Eels, Negatives, Chemistry, Say, Granite, Khaki, Lava, Size.

1 = B, 2 = E, 3 = F, 4 = A, 5 = X, 6 = M, 7 = Q, 8 = U, 9 = I, 10 = P, 11 = S, 12 = L, 13 = R, 14 = T, 15 = C, 16 = D, 17 = N, 18 = Y, 19 = G, 20 = W, 21 = O, 22 = V, 23 = H, 24 = Z, 25 = J, 26 = K.

The letters which you find from these numbers spell out the name of MOIRA CAMERON, the very first woman Yeoman Warder.

2

TOWER VISITORS

Albert / Thursday / Guide / French
Brigitte / Monday / Tourist / English
Charles / Friday / Coach driver / Spanish
Denise / Tuesday / Photographer / Italian
Eric / Wednesday / Teacher / Danish

3

HAND OVER

There were eleven Yeoman Warders on duty.

4

BACK AND FORTH

1 Warder * Redraw, **2** Keep * Peek, **3** Yard * Dray, **4** Live * Evil,
5 Doom * Mood, **6** Flow * Wolf, **7** Star * Rats, **8** Reward * Drawer.

5

STARTING WITH THE RAVEN...

1 Robin, **2** Plover, **3** Linnet, **4** Osprey, **5** Vulture, **6** Albatross.

6

THE BELL TOWER

90 minutes or an hour and a half. If he was woken by the single chime at quarter past twelve, then six more single chimes will take the time to 1.45. After a sequence of seven single chimes the only possibility is that the time is a quarter to two. He doesn't need to wait for a double chime to announce that it's two o'clock.

7

CEREMONY OF THE KEYS

Six.

CHAPTER TWELVE

GHOSTS AND ABSOLUTE LEGENDS

1

BEHEADING

Across: 6 Siberia/Iberia, 7 Flute/Lute, 9 Grumble/Rumble,
10 Sports/Ports, 12 Breed/Reed, 13 Sliver/Liver, 17 Shovel/Hovel,
18 Cheat/Heat, 21 Struck/Truck, 22 Straits/Traits, 24 Share/Hare,
25 Learned/Earned.

Down: 1 Presumed/Resumed, 2 Climb/Limb,
3 Equipped/Quipped, 4 Shears/Hears, 5 Braise/Raise,
8 Presidents/Residents, 11 Bark/Ark, 14 Crockery/Rockery,
15 Abetting/Betting, 16 Late/Ate, 19 Mother/Other,
20 Bought/Ought, 23 Madam/Adam.

2

TURN OF THE SCREW

270 turns. The large wheel makes 11 movements to complete a circle.
A number needs to be found that can be divisible by 11, 9, 6 and 5.
The lowest is 2,970. Divide this by the number of cogs on the biggest
wheel to arrive at the answer (2,970 ÷ 11 = 270).

3

DICEY

Two dots appear. (Be warned, we did say it was a dodgy dice!) The flattened-out dice gives the only possible combination there can be.

4

EXIT ROUTE

The letters scrawled on the prison wall have had their horizontal lines removed. When replaced they guide Lady Bird to her exit route. The stages of her escape are: DUNGEON, CELLAR, HALL, CHAPEL, TOWER GREEN, GATE.

5

SKULLDUGGERY

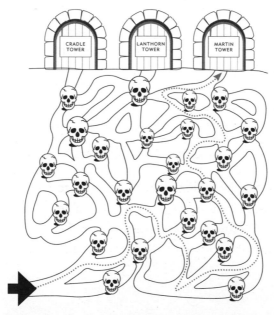

A route passing only one skull leads to Martin Tower.

6

NOW YOU SEE IT ...

1 Fort, **2** Night, **3** Age, **4** Bell, **5** Live.

7

STARE-WELL

In this puzzle it really was up to you to decide. The stairs can go either way.

CONCLUSION

1

QUIZ CROSSWORD

Across: 7 Palace, 9 Oliver, 10 Knighthood, 11 Bess, 12 Medal, 13 Catherine, 16 Crowned, 21 Betrayers, 22 Queen, 24 Jane, 25 Beefeaters, 26 Armour, 27 Dudley.

Down: 1 Haunted, 2 Hangman, 3 Jetty, 4 Gold, 5 Gilbert, 6 Peasant, 8 Yeoman Warders, 14 Heel, 15 Grey, 17 Remarry, 18 Freedom, 19 Custody, 20 Learned, 23 Heads, 25 Bury.

2

TOWER TEASERS

a) The occupations can all be made from the top line of a QWERTY keyboard, as can the names POPPY and TERRY and the name TOWER.

b) Their favourite attraction at the Tower is the RAVENS. Their names are made from letters in the word RAVEN.

c) Yeoman MARTIN shares his name with one of the towers of the Tower, and this is reflected in his lifestyle with reference to names of towers: Middle, Constable, Salt, White, Brick, Flint, Bell, Well, Wardrobe.

ACKNOWLEDGEMENTS

And so, as the Ceremony of the Keys gets underway, and as the ravens tuck into their special meals of biscuits and blood, it is time to thank the brilliant archivists and staff at the Tower of London who have done so much to make the palace an extraordinarily engaging place to visit, summoning distant centuries back into view with astounding detail. In addition to this, countless regal salutations must be paid to Roy and Sue Preston who – with Elizabethan cryptic ingenuity – have devised puzzles of such dazzling variety and brilliance; to Katie Packer, who oversaw all aspects of the book with the responsible panoptic eye of a Constable of the Tower; to Anna Herve, whose exactitude in copyediting would have won warm approval from that ferocious Keeper of Records William Prynne; to Grace Paul, whose scrutiny with proofs was as careful as that of the astronomer John Flamsteed mapping the stars; to Jessica Farrugia, publicising with all the terrific flair of Sir Walter Raleigh on the Tower ramparts; to Anna Power, a flashing crown jewel among agents; and to Sarah Emsley, whose majestic inspiration made the book possible in the first place.

Discover more ingenious brainteasers from bestselling author
Sinclair McKay to put your mind to the test . . .

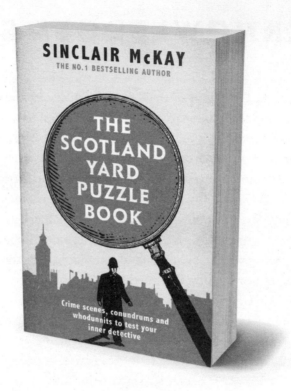

Pit your wits against the brilliant minds of Scotland Yard.

Since it opened its doors in 1829, Scotland Yard has used
the science of detection to solve the most macabre of
murders and catch the most audacious of thieves.
The Scotland Yard Puzzle Book takes a look through the
history of this famous institution and recreates some of
the most complex puzzles its detectives have ever faced.

Do you have what it takes to be
a Scotland Yard detective?

All Sinclair McKay's books are available
in paperback and as ebooks

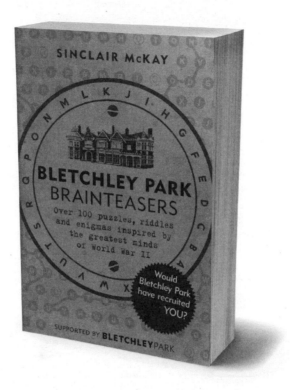

Could you have outsmarted an Enigma machine?

The Bletchley Park recruiters left no stone unturned when
searching for the best code-breakers in the land. To assess
the individuals they found they devised various ingenious
mind-twisters – hidden codes, cryptic crosswords, secret
languages, complex riddles – and it is puzzles like these,
together with the fascinating recruitment stories that
surround them, that make up this book.

Would Bletchley Park have recruited YOU?